# Spanish Highs

Also by Wayne Anthony:

*Class of 88: The True Acid House Experience*

# Spanish Highs

## Sex, Drugs & Excess in Ibiza

*Wayne Anthony*

First published in Great Britain in 1999 by Virgin Books
an imprint of Virgin Publishing
Thames Wharf Studios
Rainville Road
London W6 9HT

A catalogue record for this book is available from the British Library.

ISBN 0 7535 0302 6

Typeset by TW Typesetting, Plymouth, Devon

Printed and bound by Mackays of Chatham PLC

To my comrades around the world

The New Age is about to become the Now Age. Forget the millennium and embrace the coming era of spiritual, mental and cosmological progression.

This is the Age of Aquarius – may the force be with you.

# Contents

# Acknowledgements

Love to my precious family for their continued support, inspiration, encouragement and love.

Good luck to the newly-weds Nicola and Jason

Thanks for generous webspace Colin and team at Performance Films of Spain – **http://theclassof88.com**

Spot on Ian Gittins and crew at Virgin

Glasses raised to future allegiances and multimedia projects, including *Class of 88: The Movie!*
and **http://www.clublife2000.com**: the future of music and technology awaits on the worldwide web.

# Author's Note

Campaigners argue that drugs evoke a false sense of reality, dismissing hard evidence which conclusively proves that lives are changing every day through drug abuse. Positive or negative, the reactions to drugs are all too real. Laughter, tears, sadness . . . no one can deny the complexity of these emotions. Then again, users or potential users may see chemicals as a shortcut to enlightenment, but, in truth, drugs take you round in huge habitual circles through uncharted realms of the brain.

This is my second book concerning the different vibrant cultures that coexist with drug use. It doesn't mean that I advocate widespread class-A abuse – I don't. Yeah, call me a hypocrite . . . You may laugh, mock or completely mug me off, and deservedly so, but my chemical days are over and, mostly, I wish they'd never started.

Reading about some of them may enable you to understand why.

I'm not sure that I necessarily like the person featured in this book, and I should know, because he's me. Or rather, he *was* me . . . in a previous life, in another generation.

Sometime we all have to grow up to face the future.

In my case, I'm only just learning to face the past.

Now, come share it with me.

# Introduction

Ibiza is the best party island in the world. Geographically placed in the wonderful, picturesque and sun-soaked Balearics, it has a thriving club scene unlike anywhere else on the globe. The aircraft-hangar-sized nightclubs are simply awesome: Privilege (Ku) – capacity 8,000; Amnesia – 6,000; Space – 2,000; Es Paradis – 3,000; Pacha – 3,000; Kaos – 2,000. And that's just the bigger clubs, which are packed solid nearly every night of the week. Ibiza has done, and does, provide a temporary home, learning place and showcase for every top DJ in the world. If success beckons in the UK, Ibiza is usually the place they will have launched or reinforced their careers.

Unlike my first book, *Class of '88 – The True Acid House Experience*, this compilation of true stories doesn't explore the origins of Ibiza's club culture, or the hierarchy of various club promoters. It doesn't provide much analysis of the growth of the scene, the different music played or the prospects for Ibiza's club scene years from now. No, instead it follows me and several like-minded adventurers – with names occasionally changed to protect the innocent – as we personally immersed ourselves in Ibiza's club life over the space of around a decade. Any educational or documentary-type reportage on Ibiza is there as a backdrop, the underlying web around which each story is spun.

This is a book of sex, drugs and Acid House. It is a personal account that may shock you, may disgust you, may inspire you. I hope it will never bore you. Who knows? It may even enlighten you.

The book epitomises varied social structures at a time in the twentieth century when drugs – both controlled and outlawed

– are rampant. Ibiza is an insane place at the best of times, and drugs feature prominently there, as they do in many other countries of the world. It's a land of organised chaos, total confusion and utter mayhem ... And that's just the first chapter!

In a mixed-up world of drugs and alcohol abuse there's no telling what might happen next. So let me be your guide. Geographically, the island is split into two. North-west, we have the port of San Antonio, a package holiday resort of bars for boozing Brits. South-east, we have Ibiza Town, a multicultural playground for the rich and people in the know. When the term 'living in the fast lane' was first devised, there was nothing like Ibiza. Nowadays, rocket ships couldn't keep up with it.

The island's club culture began before the Acid House outbreak in 1987/8. In fact, this tiny island triggered off the entire Ecstasy explosion in the UK. You'll find an assortment of people in this book, as you would on the island. Step this way for famous and infamous DJs, promoters, villains, drug smugglers, dealers, Johnny Tourists, hippies, holiday reps, sexual psychotics and other unique, unforgettable characters. If *Class of '88* documented the emotions, trials, tribulations and inner thoughts of a country in the grip of recession, whilst evolving into a love-based society of open-minded conscious-ness, then *Spanish Highs* is about living for the moment.

There are those who say that the Ibiza Moment has passed, but don't you believe it. Just get out there and experience the Balearic Islands yourself. But if you can't afford the air fare, or don't fancy the risk of permanently scrambling your brain or bank balance (not to mention dress sense!), then just read on. It's a mad journey – and I took it. Amazingly, and luckily, I also came back to tell you the stories ... I'll leave it up to you to decide whether I came back in one piece!

# Spanish Highs

# 1 Like a Virgin

Nineteen eighty-eight was a somewhat unstable year for me, as a 21-year-old on the threshold of manhood, with bigger things to come. Where others might opt for a fiendish pursuit of the adolescent lifestyle, with an emphasis on the opposite sex, I chose drugs. Or maybe drugs chose me. My memory is still excellent, but somehow has an intriguing little habit of forgetting those sorts of details.

It was like this . . .

My relationship with my girlfriend of some standing was in tatters, and I stood practically alone in the vain hope of repairing the deep incisions in my soon-to-be battle-worn heart, something that had already become ominously reliant on some form of stimulus. Money did nothing to soften the blow, or fulfil my urgent needs, as I slowly slipped further into a farcical but forceful world of contention, materialism . . . and class-As.

In those days, money primarily provided a means by which I could escape from myself, not anybody else. Class-As provided a high-powered physiological vehicle to run for and drive away in at every opportunity. My once flawless friendship with my two dearest friends had also begun to falter. They couldn't bear to stand by and watch me 'kill' myself, as they put it, although that wasn't how it seemed to me. So, in keeping with my newly found consumer values, I went out and bought some new friends, who were more than happy to comply.

The origins of my excursion through the past decade of hazy chemical confusion are rooted not in Ibiza, but in the Canary island of Tenerife. The differences between the two are considerable: most people who go to Tenerife have never been to Ibiza, and vice versa. But I was in desperate need of a revitalising break in 1988 and so was my oldest buddy Keith (you may remember him from *Class of '88*). We chose this tiny island instead of Ibiza because we heard the parties were happening big time. Keith had visited the Balearics a few years previously and didn't rate the gaff.

We decided to go one day and simply left the next, without booking a hotel in advance, which meant a search for accommodation when we landed. A short taxi ride from the airport threw up Playa de Las Americas, a beachside tourist resort made up of bars, hotels, restaurants and holiday apartment complexes. It would do. The driver took us to an area called the Veronicas, a neon-lit holidaymaker's golden mile of bars and clubs. It was an 18–30 oasis for youngsters out to get completely drunk whilst maintaining a motivated sex drive, until the inevitable concluding moment of losing consciousness somewhere roadside.

Ecstasy cost £20–£25 a tab, so not that many people had heard of it or took it. Only the bods who thought they knew the score took E, which left Johnny Tourist to drink the island dry. We jumped out of the cab with our luggage outside Bananas, a suitable niterie and perhaps, looking back, a metaphor for my fragile, deceptively youthful state of mind.

Music blared from everywhere. I remember hearing the chorus from S-Express, 'Got the hots for you. I got the hots for you', as adrenaline rushed to our heads. We looked at each other with eyebrows raised.

'This is the gaff, mate!'

Soon enough we waved down another taxi, which took us round the local hotels. They were all fully booked. Luckily, the driver was able to find us another hotel in Los Cristianos, about fifteen minutes away from Playa de Las Americas. We ordered a twin suite and crashed out for the night in anticipation of the festivities ahead. These were good, exciting times.

The next morning we went in search of some gear. The first port of call had to be the Veronicas, the string of daytime bars and restaurants lining the beach front. Before we landed we'd been told that this was where to score: it was just a case of being extra-vigilant. We sat down to eat in an open-air restaurant with a clear view of the strip. Whilst knocking back the munch, we noticed two girls making themselves busy, appearing to know lots of different people. I called one of them over to our table, asking if she could help us out, or at least point us in the right direction. We guessed right, as I knew we would.

She introduced us to a soapy-looking English geezer from up North. He reminded me of a scag-head, face really pale and drawn. He beckoned us over to a sky-blue BMW. We jumped into the dirty motor, and to our bemusement an arsenal of weapons – including a kitchen knife, hammer, iron bar and a few empty bottles – littered the floor.

'Get much trouble here, then?' we asked, incredulous.

'Yeah, it goes off all the time 'ere, mate,' came the disinterested reply. 'What you after, then?'

'An eighth of Charlie, five pills and an ounce of rocky. If it's any good we'll be back.'

The girls told us the best clubs to go to and suggested we met up later for a drink in the Bandit Bar. No sooner had the taxi stopped on the strip than we found ourselves surrounded by English people head-hunting tourists to drink in the bars they represented. Calling themselves PRs (and deservedly so), they offered a series of alcoholic discounts if you accompanied the blaggers to their place of work. These English youngsters (mostly) usually lived on the island for the summer season, or sometimes all year round. Most of them were well clued-up to the best bars to visit or parties to attend, and so were worth encouraging. Many were Londoners; a few came from towns or cities such as Newcastle, Wrexham and Weymouth.

Once you're committed to running the gauntlet of 40 or more bars, represented by at least 150 people on a stretch of road of no more than 500 yards, you're accosted from every which direction: an endless corridor of tanned and pale faces giving it their best shot.

On the whole each encounter is treated in a friendly manner, but then 'No' never means no, and punters as well as PRs can sometimes adopt negative, confrontational attitudes. So you have to be careful. It's a two-way street: the workers are out there trying to earn a crust, having to adopt the role of psychologist and enter each negotiation on the same level as the punter. It's not easy by a long shot and can occasionally rub a tired workaholic up the wrong way, leaving punters on the blunt side. The flip-side is that the easy-going punter on holiday can quickly harden into an individual who'll totally ignore or dismiss any approach, maybe even threatening a few PRs along the way. Like I say, it's worth getting to know some of them, sometimes . . .

Bandit Bar was a trendy bar where punters made an effort to look fashionable, a small place but a useful location for people in the know to begin their evening before moving on. That night, we couldn't miss the girls, dressed to the nines, lapping up the admiration. After a delightful ten minutes of hugging, kissing and exchanging names, we got down to the serious business of sniffing and drinking. The girls literally knew everyone and continued to introduce us to various people throughout the night, including an Oscar-winning actress who was so down-to-earth that it felt like we'd known her for years.

We left the Bandit and our entourage moved on to Bobby's Bar, another hip gaff that played lusciously cool tunes. One of the girls' names was Paula – an attractive English girl, who looked Italian and had certainly lived and travelled the world. She insisted on meeting us again, back home, to show us the party ropes and London's thriving club scene.

Later that night, in Bananas, we both swallowed our first pill. The excitement of actually doing it was heightened by the fact that we were in a nightclub on foreign turf. On the other hand, hours seemed to pass without any related symptoms: no rushes, no warm feelings to others, nothing. Keith didn't show any signs, either . . . Our initial response was to say, 'Fuck Ecstasy, we'll stick with the sniff.'

The next day we rented a big apartment and went on a sniff-and-booze binge, which lasted two long weeks. I'd arranged to meet a dealer that night on the Veronicas: the clubs are set back from a main road with a street directly in front of them. You drive in at one end and have to drive round a blind bend under a tunnel to get out. I reached the plot at 1 a.m., but, although it was very busy, the bod was nowhere to be seen. I had a few drinks to myself outside a bar playing 'Acid Man' by Jolly Roger. Fed up with meeting different dealers, we'd organised an ounce to last the rest of the holiday. It cost £950, not much cheaper than at home and not even as good quality.

An hour passed slowly before I decided to shoot off. I drove round the tunnel, cursing the prat for messing up our plans, and hurtled straight into a Guardia Civil roadblock. Armed guards surrounded the car and instantly pulled me out. Two of them searched the motor, whilst another told me to empty my pockets on to the bonnet. Another two cars behind me were also stopped, so the soldiers were wandering from vehicle to vehicle, eager for a find.

I pulled the money out first and the soldier snatched it from my hands. 'How much in Spanish?' he grumbled in broken English.

I told him I didn't know: he kept the money in his hand and motioned for me to continue emptying my trousers. I put my right hand into the back right pocket and pulled out a packet of ripped cigarette papers! Oh bollocks . . .

In one movement of my arm I put the packet back into the pocket. The soldier knew he'd seen something, so he called for assistance from the other officers. He walked round to my left side and put his hand into the back pocket. Empty-handed, the Guardia showed his colleagues my wad of money. They started squabbling in Spanish. If they found the Rizlas, our party fund was in danger of being confiscated on the grounds of my being a suspected drug dealer, and I could even have got bashed up.

I put my hand into the back right pocket and transferred the papers into the front pocket they'd previously searched, but the soldiers were so wrapped up in conversation about the dosh that none of them noticed what I had done. Suddenly, they stopped arguing. One of them came to my right side and searched the now-empty pocket. The original chap who searched me looked bewildered; he knew something was afoot, but for some reason didn't bother searching me again. The obvious question being: Why was I carrying this amount of sterling?

Of course, I told them that I was on holiday with my girlfriend, who didn't like leaving it in the apartment. I really got the impression they were thinking of keeping it, but could find no good reason to. The squaddie Dibble resentfully handed me the money, and gave me a stern warning about drink-driving. I couldn't apologise enough ... I know what bastards some of them could be – they could easily take you into the mountains and beat the living shit out of you.

Since landing we'd heard some horrific stories of the English being beaten up by the Guardia. One day, we'd met some girls who had nowhere to stay: they'd spent the last two nights on the beach. Their stuff was left with some friends in an apartment, but there wasn't enough space for them to kip. There were three girls staying with us by now anyway, so two more wasn't gonna hurt. Not that they were street girls or anything; they were spotlessly clean and spent most of the year travelling to exotic locations. They really looked after us and would do anything to keep us happy. I took them to collect their clothes from the friend's apartment some fifteen minutes away. We reached the complex only to discover the apartment empty – there wasn't a suitcase in sight. We hurried into the main reception to ask the manager if he could check the safe for their passports. He told us to wait five minutes, pointing at some chairs for us to rest our weary bones on.

Minutes later, screeching brake-pads and burning rubber announced the arrival of the Guardia Civil, who came steaming into the building. Immediately the manager pulled two passports from a drawer, before handing them to the captain, who resembled Saddam Hussein. It turned out that the fellas with the girls' suitcases had disappeared in the early hours, owing shitloads of rent. The girls told the officer in charge they'd not long known the vanishing occupants and had left them in charge of their luggage.

We were promptly arrested and taken to a police station near the beach front. Our original holiday budget and stash had been exhausted in the first few days, so I'd planned to visit the bank after collecting their stuff, which was why I was carrying my passport and credit cards. I'd lost a passport six months previously, and had picked up an emergency replacement from Petty France (at St James's Park in London) for the trip. Although I still had the freedom of travel, the passport was only valid for one year, but on my return from holiday it could be stamped for the remaining nine years. The Guardia found this strange and accused me of carrying a forged document of travel. They asked where we were staying, so I told them Los Cristianos. He asked if anyone else was in the apartment at that moment. I said everyone was on the beach and they had the apartment keys. I was sponning so much I should have been wearing a porkie-pie hat.

The miserable officers frog-marched us into what resembled a police charge-room. I was immediately handcuffed to a wooden chair. Having your hands cuffed behind your back is a particularly unnerving experience and leaves you completely vulnerable to unprovoked attack by the aggressors. The room was smelly, filthy and in urgent need of repair. There were two cheap desks leaning up against the wall, a load of papers stacked on a bookshelf, some rusty filing cabinets and what looked like a cell door over in the corner. The Guardia must have been allergic to water, cos they smelt like shit, sweltering in hot sunshine. I don't know why, but for some reason they didn't like me one iota. One of the guards stood menacingly over me, while the others asked questions. I glared into his eyes and the bastard slapped me hard round the face. I went into one, declaring that I was a British citizen who had done nothing wrong. A clenched fist came from way back, connecting with my chin. Rough justice?

I remember being dragged off the floor. The same guy had me by the throat and was shouting at me to shut the fuck up. Because I refused to acknowledge his command, he dug sharp fingernails into my Adam's apple. The girls' cries of 'Let go!' went unheard, and until I nodded my head he wouldn't loosen his grip. They decided to search the beach for our mates, and then search the apartment. Looking like some particularly unpleasant extras from *Midnight Express*, they escorted me down to one end of the beach before letting me go ahead alone, with a warning, to track down the door keys. I knew we had drugs back at the gaff: about a quarter-ounce of Charlie and two ounces of puff. I just couldn't take the Guardia back there: Keith was home and would have been nicked too.

I slowly walked along the beach, pretending to look in all directions. As soon as I was out of sight, I ran over to a taxi rank by the side of the road. When I reached the apartment, I held the taxi and ran upstairs, banging on the door. Keith answered.

'Quickly, Dibble are on their way. Get rid of everything in the gaff!'

I rushed back to the cab and then on to the beach: it took around 20 minutes. I walked back along the beach to where the jeep had been parked, but melted rubber marked the vacant spot. I continued to the station, and immediately an armed desk sergeant grabbed me and sat me down, handcuffing my hands to the chair. I could hear muffled sounds coming from the cell door, and two minutes later three muscle-bound officers came out of the cell. The door opened just enough for me to spot the Charlie dealer we'd first bought our gear from. The poor chap was lying on the floor covered in claret: we made eye contact and I gave him a sly nod. The door slammed shut, echoing around the building and inside my head like the opening sequence of *Porridge*. My balls of steel (what?!) had shrunken into small pellets; fear began to grasp my soul. These guys were fucking dangerous.

The jeep came screeching to a halt outside, and four soldiers jumped out. Wham! I was struck again; my face was bruised, with blood pouring from my lip.

'You are clever, English man, no?' one of them sneered.

'Why are you holding us? We've done nothing wrong.'

'Why you get taxi?'

'What taxi?'

'You want we hurt you again?'

'Course not!'

Instantly, the girls switched tactics: instead of yelling at the hit-squad, their natural feminine qualities came into play, defusing an escalating situation that wasn't going in my favour. One of them explained that we were friends from back home and that I was only trying to help them get their stuff back. The officer reeled off a string of the saddest English-language chat-up lines ever imagined. He was, amazingly, totally relaxed about it: if he were portraying a man with the sophistication of Lawrence of Arabia, he'd have got a flippin' Oscar. More embarrassingly, he began to divulge interesting personal information, which could have been very handy if it got into the wrong hands.

Two months from then, he rambled, he'd be working in London, based at Paddington nick for twelve weeks. It was some annual exchange deal with the British Old Bill. With all the Cockney of a pearly king, I told her to find out where and when he was coming and to give him her number, so that she could be contacted when he arrived. The guards had really hurt me, my face was badly bruised, and dried blood stuck to my cheeks, chin and neck. If payback was in order, I had just the forfeit: a big ugly black queen nicknamed FF!

He suddenly snapped at me.

'Where you go in taxi?'

'My friends weren't on the beach. I didn't want to get into more trouble. So l went home to make sure someone was there. I tried to be as quick as I could,' I blathered.

'You are lucky. The taxi says you only stop for two minutes. If longer, God cannot help you. We see your friends and search the apartment. I let you go only because she is nice and we meet in London.'

None of us needed telling twice. The soldier who kept digging me grabbed my arm and glared into my eyes. Knowing I could physically do this motherfucker didn't stop me from looking at the ground. Unfortunately she gave Saddam the wrong telephone number, because she was afraid of comebacks. The soldier said I was lucky (wow!) . . . If only he knew.

Two months later Paula called me to say she'd be flying into London for one night, before jetting off to Ibiza. We arranged to meet outside Victoria station later that night: she'd planned to show us a club called Future at Heaven in Charing Cross. We were smart dressers and turned up in Gaultier/Armani suits. Once our friendship was reinforced on British soil, Keith, Paula and I made our way to the club and parked at the back of the station. On the approach to the arches I spotted some graffiti painted on the wall – BADLANDS – and an arrow pointing in the direction of the club.

Inside, brilliant, blinding stage-cans shone directly at us, causing temporary loss of sight. After regaining partial vision, large shapes of nine or ten doormen began to appear, with snarling Rottweilers and Dobermans on chain-link leads. We were searched in a fashion not far short of a police class-A rub-down. Their aim was intimidation: to scare the living shit out of dealers and users – and it worked.

However, once past this stronghold and into the club, I felt more relaxed than I had in ages. We almost went into shock when passing the packed dance floor, for people were dancing and screaming 'Ecstasy!' at the top of their voices. The Tears for Fears track 'Shout' was playing at full blast. I looked around this room and immediately felt out of place in my suit. If Paula hadn't known the promoters, we'd never have got in, because the door policy was very strict. It seemed as if everyone was looking at us, knowing this was our first time.

I felt like Dixon of Dock Green ('Hello, hello, hello, what we got here then?'). Everyone else was wearing T-shirts, bandannas and ripped jeans: most of them sported a tan and could have come straight from the beach. The atmosphere was like nothing I had ever seen before, never mind felt. Although at that point I'd never been to the States, I imagined it would be just like this (later, after going to the US, I realised the Americans were on a totally different trip by 1988). But the whole Ecstasy phenomenon took a new turn when it reached these shores. Paul Oakenfold – then a mere up-and-coming DJ – was playing a specialised set of Balearic, dance and rock music. The electric energy and aura of those sweaty dancing bodies illuminated the entire club. It was like every last person ultimately felt the incredible vibe. I'd never seen a female DJ until Nancy Noise stepped up to the decks and gave it hell. It was an eye-opening night . . .

I knew I'd be back with a vengeance the following week, and I was.

# **2** Space Cadets

Some people just don't know when to quit or call it a night, or should I say day. They push their endurance levels well past breaking point with a limitless supply of alcohol, quiver, pills and trips. This lot call themselves 'the weekend crew', and rightly so, except that the parties extend beyond the allocated 48 hours of Saturdays and Sundays. In Ibiza, every day heralded another action-packed evening of first-class entertainment. The weekend crew had been out for more than 24 hours, huddling together like a duck with her ducklings. They didn't speak in quacks, but had their own secret language, tone and humour, which only a fellow-buzzer could understand: in-jokes, private references, you know the stuff.

Anyway, this one night in '95 the crew were all on a mission of utter self-destruction. The next port of call, it was decided, would be 'Space', and although it was too early for the terrace bar to open (at 10 a.m.), a right old knees-up was in order. An assortment of characters from various fields in the entertainment industry made the group both interesting and, unsurprisingly, obnoxiously big-headed, with not a single regard for anyone around them. None the less, they were very tight amongst their own, whacked out on another planet but still aware of their like-minded buddies and in close proximity at most, if not all, times.

A long corridor separated the morning sun from the techno-heaven enclosed in fog-bound darkness. Repressions tended to be left at the entrance, as a congregation from the gay community ran rampant and free within these walls. It was funny how the tables were turned, and in a direct inversion of (then, certainly) society's normal codes, it was the heterosexuals, and even some homosexuals, who were intimidated or even bullied by overbearing factions of the 'I'm against anything that isn't loudly gay' fanatics. The vibes towards anyone who objected to anything going down were decidedly not good.

At its best, every day is Mardi Gras in Ibiza. Space had been transformed into the most prestigious fashion capital in Europe, a shrine for flamboyant lesbians, heterosexuals, homosexuals, transsexuals, cross-dressers and bisexuals to party in until the light of day, in outfits still sweaty from the night before. Once upon a time it had been the Mediterranean's best-kept secret, but – like the island itself – was no longer exclusively inhabited by locals, gays, millionaires and their entourages. As Ibiza had blossomed into the world's most glamorous party island, so the tourist economy had boomed, as had drug use.

This one night, however, the normally limitless supply of narcotics had all but run out. There'd been some Chas flying about, but it had quickly been seen to by gold cards digging into the stash. My own battle-wearied hooter was, unsurprisingly, numb after an assault not far short of Bosnia had raged around my nostrils. When it came to tooting, I have to admit that in my heyday I was up there with the best of them, and the one thing I could easily sniff out was any moody gear. I'd probably have been a sniffer dog if I could have found a collar to fit me: put it this way, there's plenty who tell me I'm already totally barking!

Anyway, I digress: the moody marching powder.

'This ain't Charlie!' I declared, as DG quickly went in search of the Yank who sold him seven wraps of dodgy gear. He found the geezer but he was totally wired, telling DG it wasn't cocaine but 'Special K', or ketamine ... which is more generally used as horse anaesthetic. Luckily DG hadn't taken it, but stupidly he was interested in trying it anyway. By the time he came back to the group, everyone was so fucked they didn't care anyway. Derrick and I couldn't hear anything, other than each other's voices, which seemed to float over the music as if in slow motion, like walking on the moon.

I called out to my long-time friend: 'Derrick, I feel funny, man!'

He did too: 'How come I can hear you over the music?'

'Dunno, mate. I can't hear anything else. Have they stopped the record?'

Neither of us was very comfortable at all with the disoriented way we were feeling but, laughing nervously in each other's faces, we scanned the club for pals. We soon spotted what looked like DG's girlfriend, Ann, lying on the deck near the dance floor. Jenny was seated next to her, watching us space-walk across the strobe-infested dance arena. Each step felt like another giant leap for mankind: it felt like we were defying gravity to cross no-man's-land into the other side. Ann was still lying down when we reached her, and I had to apologise for not being in any sort of fit state to help the damsel in distress to her feet. Instead, not wanting our pal's missus to feel left out, we also sat on the floor, laughing and joking about the cocoon-like dimensions of our bananas buzz. Ann told us she'd never experienced anything like this K-hole before and said she could see 360 degrees around her: like a narcotic witch of Eastwick, she tried guessing what clubbers standing at the bar behind her were wearing. She didn't get any right, but it did keep us entertained for ages!

When we landlubbers rose to attention the club seemed to have filled with people. We were soon separated, and so I wandered alone in search of the gang. I knew this drug was far more dangerous than it seemed, because by this time I could only stare at the ground. If I looked anywhere else, people's flippin' faces were fiercely vibrating! Seated against the wall at the back of the club, I became scared and frightened. Voices in my mind whispered words without any meaning. A group of guys glared across the room: they were gay and aggressively proud of it, you could tell. Suddenly I started feeling paranoid. In a flash I wanted to run like hell towards the exit, but feared they'd block my path.

Trying to remain calm, I stood up, back still firmly against the wall. For a horrible void of five or so minutes I stood plotting my escape route. The thing was, I didn't even know if I was right to be worried, I was so off my head. But I did know that if anyone laid a hand on me, I would have fought to the death to escape: all I needed was to reach the light, where my friends would see the pitched battle and come to lend a hand. It didn't feel as if human beings were against me, but the powerful slaves of some dark, psychotic demon. It felt like *Omen III*.

Convinced that everybody in the club was out to get me, I was all prepared for a violent counter-attack, when I suddenly glimpsed the figure of a pal I hadn't seen for years, stopping me in my tracks. It was my black mate Keith. He had bright green eyes which you can spot a mile off.

'Keith, I'm in trouble here. Help me, will ya?'

Like leading a distressed child, Keith took me outside on to the terrace. It was a completely different atmosphere there, and the crowds were going barmy. The music banged out by Alex P & Brandon Block (Peezy and Blocko) electrified the punters, who were dancing in all the available spaces. Immediately I felt at ease and safe amongst the predominantly mixed clubbers, despite the fact that I was wearing a sarong, which would often attract ribbing or unwanted attention. I loved my sarong and can easily understand why David Beckham was prepared to look a plonker in one in the tabloids. It was the most comfortable item of clothing I'd ever had the balls to wear. The girls loved it too: it showed an open mind as well as a chilled-out attitude. As I stood on the terrace, though, some black guys were staring and giggling at me, while at the same time their girlfriends smiled secretly and clearly appreciated my good taste.

Suddenly one of the guys approached me.

'Hey, man. Why d'you wear a skirt?'

Instantaneously I was concerned again. Like a pack of hyenas on heat, his pals watched closely as their nominated spokesperson made contact. I asked if he thought all black people were African descendants, and as soon as he replied 'Yes', I asked why, then, did all their African brothers wear skirts. Stumped and confused, the potential aggressor walked away lost in thought.

The DJs played anthem after anthem to the hyper-pleased shrieks of the whole terrace. Space was directly situated on the flight path to Evissa airport, just around the corner. The aeroplanes flying overhead were part of Space's charismatic

karma. Every now and then an aircraft would fly over in time
with the DJ's mix, at which moment the clubbers under the
influence responded with a roar of applause. The other,
drug-free ravers would join in too, although they didn't know
why they were clapping. It was fantastic and I was buzzing
beyond my usual control.

Some time later I went outside to the car park, where the DJ
Norris Windross was in a state of some hysteria, kicking in the
headlights on my hired car. I took a run-up and returned the
compliment by drop-kicking one of the doors in Windross's
Renault. Madness prevailed, as the rest of the clan piled out of
the terrace and began wrecking each other's motors. I couldn't
believe it! There was I, pounding all the panels on three of my
mates' vehicles, whilst sixteen-stone Adam Englander –
aka Virgina Man – practised trampoline techniques on the
others! The clubbers stood amazed as we potatoed cavemen
smashed, broke and scratched our way around the car park.
Security – understandably, because we must've seemed like a
right bunch of nutters – didn't want to get involved and left us
to our own devices. We in turn found the carnage so funny that
we were having trouble standing up. Pissed, drugged up and
like bulldozers in a china shop, things went from bad to
dramatically worse as Mark jumped in his motor to escape the
wrecking crew, and at that very moment a DJ, carrying record
boxes, walked by the car, which slammed into reverse. The
place was carnage!

The mixer extraordinaire shot up in the air, landing on the
boot before crumpling on to the floor. The entire car park held
its breath as the DJ somehow sprang to his feet with both hands
in the air, gathered the boxes and continued walking towards
his vehicle. Mobbed by the whole crew, he was forced to sit
down for a while. Whatever was keeping him from agony was
certainly not natural sedatives.

Mark gave him a number of bribes, including Es, sniff and
£50 in order to ease his 'landing'. Once the dust had settled it
was agreed to make the hazardous journey to the Kanya Bar
and see our old mate Tony Oneto. But before anyone could get
into the scrapheaps, a gleaming Peugeot 306 convertible drove
by at 5 m.p.h. The driver, Aaron, was running crazily after the

empty vehicle shouting at it to stop. Loony tunes erupted once more as the entourage of 20 played bumper cars from one end of the island to the other. Bloomin' scraped potatoes, the lot of us!

Kanya Bar was another sunset cafe, located on the same coastline as Cafe del Mar and Mambo's in San Antonio, and within five minutes' walking distance of them both. In those days Kanya was on an underground speed-garage tip, so it remained in the shadow of the commercially known sunset cafés (although now that looks like changing). There was a swimming pool scattered with sunbeds, for lounging, and a shaded area for eating. The technics were set in a small wooden shed, positioned in a corner near the pool. A six-foot fence of bamboo protected the equipment from direct sunlight.

Like a bunch of escaped animals, we spontaneously ignited a full-on party. The DJs – Owen Clark, Norris Windross, Alex P, Brandon Block, Dominic Spreadlove, Tony Oneto, Nigel Benn (who'd come to play at Kaos) and Tony Trax – played on rota for more than eight hours. Before long the café was packed solid, with nutters going for it everywhere. The infamous Sunrise promoter Tony Colston-Hayter even paid a visit, but unfortunately fell drunk down six concrete steps and practically broke his ankle! But even that didn't stop the barmy entrepreneur climbing to his feet and starting to jump up and down on the weakened joint, before falling painfully to the ground. Then someone stepped on his hand and broke two fingers, but Tony boldly (or bananas-ly!) refused hospital treatment. He eventually left the island with a busted rib, broken fingers and a badly sprained ankle. Oddly enough, he didn't remember how it had happened. Acid House promoters, still catching headlines. Some things never change!

Meanwhile, back at Kanya, a discarded cigarette had started a fire behind the fence by the DJ shed. The punters were pouring their drinks over it until the owner drenched the flames with a few buckets of water. At this point, one of my good friends, 'Stretch', came searching for me at the Kanya Bar to take me to a party being held by one of the fashion industry's leading model agents. All the top models were flown to the island specifically for this event, and Stretch had managed to secure several bonzer names on the guest list. We had to be carefully selected, highly suitable nominees capable of holding our own in the company of such glamorous people . . . So why he chose me is beyond me! Only kidding. The applicants were promptly vetted and we were told to meet in an hour's time.

The motion of the car and the slipstream of air hit me head-on whilst I sat in the back of the BMW convertible. It was a cause for some concern, as my eyes spun like cricket balls inside their sockets. Three bottles of Jack Daniels, twelve bottles of champagne, countless chapitos, ten pills, the Special K and three grams – I was knackered! I re-entered the warmth of my own villa. Stretch was a little worried about me, but had been out with me hundreds of times and knew I could be nutty. Once I'd showered and had a change of clothes, his friend would feel much better – or so he thought. Stretch left, promising to return within the hour to pick me up, but I was fucked. The room span so fast I couldn't stand up without puking. I made it up a few times, though, enough to bring up the alcohol-based fluid doing what for in my stomach.

Normally I'm a hygienic sort of bod. I hate public toilets: it's not so bad when you just want a piss, but normally I'd wipe the entire toilet basin before covering it with toilet paper and sitting down. But here all hygienic procedures were cancelled, as I crouched on my knees, cuddling the cold enamel, with my face resting on the wet rim. Water poured from my eyes to join the streams of sweat dripping from my gonzered body. I couldn't see, move or speak, except to moan and groan with considerable discomfort. There was nothing but alcohol and pills in my belly, so most of the heaving only brought up small amounts of what looked liked pure JD. My throat was red raw and my tonsils had turned into basketballs with thorns. God help anybody who tries to film this!

I lay wide awake on my back, soaked from head to foot in perspiration. Stretch saw me first and got everyone out of the villa so that no one could take pictures of his friend. Top Bloke. He knew there was no way I was gonna make it to the gig. After spraying me with cold water, Stretch carried me over and laid me on the bed. He felt confident I'd recover after some much-needed kip, so he slipped off and went on to the party.

Meanwhile I'd fallen into noisy sleep, waking several hours later when my friends returned buzzing from the party. They ambiguously told of wild supermodel exploits (which, surprisingly enough, later turned out to be true) before they went to sleep. I was gutted . . . and still awake.

Desperate for some – any – piece of the action, I drove to the Croissant Show in Ibiza Town, bumping into a few of clubland's better-known personalities. They had three groupies in tow and insisted I should go to their villa with them . . . The job sounded a good one.

As soon as we walked through the door, a bag of Charlie was hurled on to the table. Richard made a pipe, and the group – barring me – started smoking rocks. There was something a bit seedy about this: the supposed 'in-crowd' piping crack, and feeling really good about it too. This was the sort of behaviour that regularly enticed silly club girls, who loved hanging out with known personalities, to join in their devilish drug orgy. These women exposed themselves to all sorts of unknown dangers just to be seen with the right people in the right places. I left them to it, letting them carry on their saddening 'party' without me, and instead returning quietly home to take a coma-inducing prescription sleeping tablet appropriately called Stilnox.

Yup, me discovering limits and even morals! Whatever fuckin' next?

# 3 True Romance

Sundays in London were never quite the same after 1992. That year, the whole Sunday clubbing concept went full circle and transformed into the high-powered industry it is today. The term 'speed garage' wasn't even invented then – it was just called garage – although the tunes would still bang on the bpm meter without some industry name giving them a specialised marketing tag.

A normal Sunday began around 2 a.m. in the VIP room at Ministry of Sound, following which the party would continue in a local (law-abiding) pub that wouldn't serve alcohol before the 11 a.m. start of the licensing hours, and from there we'd usually crowd up another pub till the clubs opened again. This cycle could continue for anything up to four days, after which even the most hard-headed party animal would have to concede that the spirit was willing, but the body was completely potatoed.

One Sunday in '93 I had to get to Gatwick airport. Tank was driving; Dominic Spreadlove, Chris Creed and Gary the doorman from Brighton were also in the car. We'd been on the razz since Friday night and were completely fucked, all systems failing after five bottles of Martell, 20-odd bottles of champagne, untold pills and a good ounce or so of nosebag. The plan was that the lads would drop me off before heading to yet another house party. It was my first trip to Ibiza and, from everyone else's stories, I was expecting a trip I'd dine out on for years to come.

Tank's reputation as a stunt driver was widely known amongst clubbers. He used to drive through town like a rally driver, a complete maniac if the truth be told. And that was just when he was sober. That Sunday he was at the wheel, knocking back alcohol like it was water, having the occasional sniff and jigging up and down in the seat to the deep, dark garage beats of Dominic's mix tape. Red traffic lights stopped the car at the junction of Vauxhall Bridge, and a green filter light indicated for cars turning right towards Victoria. Tank slipped into the outside lane and drove straight across the main road, on the brink of carnage, as onlookers and a policeman on a motorbike glared open-mouthed. Panic ripped through the motor. We couldn't believe what Tank had just done.

The copper was all over us like a rash, and we're there with coke, booze, puff and four drunk passengers on board! Blue flashing neons reflected on the interior roof. Tank pulled over, telling us not to worry, he'd sort it, and he jumped out to meet the officer. We thought the end was nigh and that we had more chance of being nicked than a bloke climbing out of a window with a bag named 'Swag' and half your father's hi-fi. I was sweating cobs. Dominic played it real cool, or as cool as someone could who was convinced that Tank was invisible. He was even laying bets that the copper wouldn't produce a breathalyser, saying this happened all the time to Tank. We were dumbfounded and thought it was on top. We called Dominic and Tank all the names under the sun.

We were gobsmacked when Tank got into the car and declared that everything was sweet.

'Are you part of some weird secret society?' I asked, incredulous.

Tank was a big fella, with gold teeth you'd spot a mile off. His breath smelt like a refinery from all of six feet. His heavy laugh vibrated the car window. As he told it, the officer had asked him if he realised what he'd just done, and Tank had said he didn't realise until it was too late. The traffic cop literally told him to fuck off. Dominic was pissing himself with laughter. He was right and we, the unbelievers, were wrong. It was a relief not to be arrested, but to this day I still wonder what exactly Tank did say to the fucker. Whatever it was, soon afterwards I was up in the skies, cruising through the kingdom of the gods on the way to the holiest land of Acid House – Ibiza.

The flight was a blast. Stuck inside a great metal bird,

exploring the astral cosmos, I sent telepathic messages to the one I loved – who was also in the skies on the way back from a week in the Balearics. Either the telepathy didn't work or she didn't love me! There were no replies.

Eventually my mind wandered to the mates who were to meet me at the airport and introduce me to the party scene. But when I got to Evissa airport there was no one there. Great start! I sat in Arrivals and felt sick to the stomach, partly cos there was no welcome, but probably also cos my insides were mashed from drugs and alcohol. Miles from home . . . What the fuck was I gonna do?

The airport was completely dead, apart from a few latecomers rushing into Departures. At the far end of the building I noticed a blonde girl heading my way, some considerable way off, her tanned skin beaming with rude health. I couldn't wait to see her face. As I stepped out for air, I looked for the search party and began to roll a fat joint. The girl was still coming, and as she walked through the automated doors I couldn't believe it – it was my girl! Boy, was I glad to see her. Turned out her Gatwick-bound plane had been delayed, so she blagged her way back through customs to see where I was. She told me where I could find my friends, saying I was to take a taxi to a club called Pacha and hook up with her pals. Minutes later she'd gone again, leaving me to roll another fat one and take in the beautiful evening air.

Suddenly there was a blast of loud music as a Cherokee jeep pulled up outside the terminal. The occupants quickly unloaded some cases and approached the entrance. I recognised one of the guys from back home. After a few brief introductions, the guy I knew insisted that I head back to the villa with his American buddies and search for my AWOL 'welcoming party' the next day. I chucked my suitcase into the jeep and we high-tailed it up to the mountains. Half an hour later we were driving through the gates of a big fuck-off Spanish villa with an Olympic-size swimming pool. Turned out the Yanks had recently graduated from Harvard and their parents had sent them on a world boating cruise and given them their own motor yacht and full crew! Nice work if you can get it.

I walked into the main living quarters and couldn't help

smiling. The place was chocka with scantily clad beauties having a race to finish off some massive lines of gear. The winner had the most amazing, hypnotic green eyes I'd ever seen, although one glance at her dream-like figure told me – this truly sad womaniser! – that if I went anywhere near it, I'd be bang in trouble and barking like a dog within minutes. Woof woof!

There wasn't even time to think about it, though, as Charlie's angels demanded I join the contest. My first attempt was marred by a few pauses but I soon got the hang of it, whacked up an enormous white line and my throat tasted like tarred sherbet. A few hours later we all hit the town in search of my missing mates.

The first stop was San Antonio. The bars and restaurants were doing a roaring trade from (mostly English) tourists getting blind drunk on cheap alcohol and making complete arses of themselves. No wonder the Spanish disliked a lot of the Brits. I can't say I blamed 'em. We walked around scores of bars, dodging the people and a punch-up, until someone called my name. It was two of Ibiza's popstar-status DJs – Peezy and Blocko. The boys were extremely merry after necking fifteen vodkas in the space of an hour. I arranged for them to meet the Yanks and tour the islands aboard their yacht a couple of days onward. We just ordered a bottle of Mescal Tequila and spent the next hour slamming and toasting friends who didn't make it. Nutters, the lot of 'em. The entire road was teeming with girls and boys out to have a good time – which meant a drunk time. I tore at the Tequila worm with my teeth and ordered a bottle of mega-strong Polish vodka. The lads were all cheering loudly, coming on to every woman who walked by and loving every minute.

Suddenly a group of guys seated next to us pulled out some club posters, talking about what fantastic DJs Peezy and Blocko were.

'But this is them,' I said, pointing to my two boozy colleagues. 'This *is* Alex Peezy and Brandon Block!'

They didn't believe me, probably because the boys didn't appear wild enough, by now too plastered even to move. Or maybe because I must sometimes seem such a bare-faced liar!

Peezy and Blocko managed drunken fits of laughter as I asked the waitress for a pen so that they could sign the poster.

Blocko's 'signature' was immensely succinct – 'Fuck off, you cunts' – while Peezy settled for a hardly more mature 'Bollocks'. The pair of them thought it was extremely funny, but the two fans didn't see the humour. In order to pacify them I offered a bet – 500 quid says they'll see this genuine 'Peezy and Blocko' that night behind the decks at Pacha. The fellas were so confident I was liaring, they even offered their girlfriends as part of the deal. Which sounded to me like a bet I just couldn't afford to lose. The only way Peezy and Blocko wouldn't turn up was if the daft sods got right at it the night before the morning after. Which, on the form I'd just witnessed, wasn't entirely out of the question.

We crawled through the crowds to reach another club called Nightlife, a smallish gaff, maybe a couple of hundred people. The DJ-owner Tony was a deep garage man, mostly into US stuff and more recently UK material. We'd only been there a short while when up came the guys who'd had the wager, their girlfriends in tow. Surprisingly, they weren't half bad-looking. Even more amazingly, after hearing what their boyfriends had planned for them, they were well up for it! (Girls are a different breed in Ibiza, as I would soon discover. Fuelled by drugs, alcohol and miles away from home, lots of them would be up for just about everything. But that would have to wait.)

Everybody left whilst I stayed with the DJs and Tony, chasing champagne with chapitos. Before long the room spun and orange clouds of smoke hung over the dancefloor. I decided I'd better leave before I passed out, which wouldn't have been much of a result on my first night. I could hear Ibiza-veteran DJs laughing at me as I stumbled into the street, hopelessly trying to walk off the horribly intense feeling of internal obliteration. Sometime later I realised the horrible truth – I'd lost the Americans' villa address and telephone number!

Eventually I sat down in a quiet road away from peering eyes and puked my entire guts out. I must have looked gross, but at least I felt better. An hour or so later I could feel my senses returning, and aimlessly wandered the streets of San Antonio trying to locate the bar again. Instead I faintly heard shouts from a balcony across the road – it was the guys and dolls. I hauled myself upward towards their invite of a spliff, but they decided it was better to come down and meet the walking brewery. Their block was under tight surveillance by a caretaker – a total fuckin' jobsworth. He wasn't gonna let *me* crash out in their apartment block. Still, I promised to be a good boy and only visit briefly, and he finally let me upstairs. One of the girls poured me a European measure of Jack Daniels, and we were all puffing on joints, when suddenly the front door crashed open. It was the raging caretaker, and he had a tooth-chompin' iron bar!

He charged into the room screaming in Spanish, raising the weapon and bringing it crashing down on top of a lampshade, just by my chair.

'Hold up, man . . . mggghh!'

I rose from the seat as the great chunk of iron became embedded in my shoulder bone. Somehow I managed to dive over the table, crashing on to the floor. Immediately the caretaker was on me, about to crack my head open, when one of the girls whacked him with a marble chopping board. My attacker fell unconscious on the ground, I grabbed her by the hand and we made a hasty exit. Of all the chat-up techniques in all the world, being rescued from someone wielding an iron bar wasn't one I fancied trying often. It had good results, though. We must have run through the quiet back streets for at least ten minutes before stopping, lost, for a rest. I thanked my bright-eyed heroine, still breathless and taken aback, but sealing this new true romance with a kiss.

The magnesium light of a taxi exploded into the darkness and we quickly flagged it down. I was pain-stricken and didn't have a clue where I was, when suddenly I remembered the name of the Americans' villa.

'Casa Blanca.' Of all the places in all the world . . .

The driver got directions from a lively radio operator. Up into the safety of the mountains we drove, laughing about what had happened mere moments ago. We reached the villa to find no one home, so I left a note and asked the driver to take us to a hotel in Ibiza Town. The cabby dropped us at one hotel, but I took the caution of going to another, in case the Guardia contacted the cab firm. You can't take any chances. We booked a double room and remained on the complex for two days, before finally feeling safe enough to visit a local Spanish bar. One morning an English resident in the hotel mentioned he was selling trips. Oh no, this could be trouble.

At 6 a.m. we – the new couple – dropped one tab each before locking ourselves in our room. We couldn't stop laughing: everything we said or did caused complete, stupid hysterics. The only shadow of reality was an increasing and insatiable craving for cigarettes, but neither of us felt capable of leaving the secure surroundings. It felt like a nuclear fall-out refuge: nothing could harm us here, not even the fast disappearing remnants of our inhibitions.

Claudia was a very pretty girl and looked a lot like my girlfriend back home. At times I thought she was her. Eventually I decided to go out and find the cigarette machine I'd vaguely glimpsed earlier. We kissed passionately, as if it was our last intimate moment together. Seconds after stepping into the corridor of matching doors, the whole hallway seemed to stretch away from me, longer and longer. I walked towards the lift area, trying to keep my composure and not run back to the room. Suddenly I found myself standing in front of the lift.

Once out of the building into the street, I concentrated on finding the machine. There it was. But as I stood in front of the dispenser with my money in my hand, I started to ponder the implications of this strategically positioned executioner. Nicotine kills thousands each year due to cancer, and here in the so-called modern world smokers are hopelessly addicted to something that can put you in an early grave. The words echoed in my mind as the coins landed in the metal box.

Death.

Cancer.

Graveyard.

Pushing the button on the machine was like signing my own death warrant. The fag packet dropped in the tray and a Wild West theme-tune blasted out from inside the machine. I jumped back in shock, looking round to see if someone was trying to trick me, but there was no one in sight. I closely examined the metal casing and put more coins into the slot. It played the same tune – a famous Clint Eastwood film soundtrack from *The Good, the Bad and the Ugly*. Death dispensed with a tune! I faced the vendor and wondered who could design such a horrific exterminator. Within seconds I wanted Claudia to share this experience and rushed back to the hotel. There she was – wrapped in a quilt – claiming she was a sausage roll! She kept this up for fifteen minutes before exploding into fits of laughter at the look on my face.

The vendor encounter was soon forgotten when the rays of sunshine engulfed the room. We decided to go for a walk in the harbour and took along a few sticks of French bread to feed the fish. We should have been more worried about whether we'd think we were fish! After carefully selecting a scenic spot on the rocks to sit down on, with our feet in the water, a feeding frenzy erupted around our toes. Now I've seen the film *Piranha* and I loved it, but I'd no desire actually to be in it. Luckily, most of the fish were only small, and didn't seem to lust after the taste of human, but every so often a great big one would appear and batter through the others in search of food.

Something – drugs, presumably – got me analysing the difference between the seemingly natural thinking of modern man and his ancient predecessors, one of the looming questions being whether survival of the fittest was a mental or physical thing. I thought about this and many other topics for ages, hardly saying a word to the girl. Sometimes I'd begin a sentence with 'Claudia, what if . . . ?' She barely caught up with me and I'm not sure she'd have wanted to. I was deep – too deep – in barmy thought and I hardly noticed the sound of a small-engined boat approaching from the distance. Suddenly an American voice yelled my name: 'Wayne, you lightweight!' It was my newly acquainted buddies in a rubber raft and on their way to their yacht, moored in the bay somewhere. They invited us on a cruise around Formentera and the other islands surrounding Ibiza. Sounded great!

However, Claudia suddenly announced that she had to be at the airport in two hours' time to meet her friends, as they were all scheduled to leave that very night. She jumped up and said she'd grab a taxi in the port and make it in time to catch them. The Guardia would never recognise her and she didn't need a passport to leave the country. She insisted I went with my mates and promised to call as soon as she landed in London. Like a fairy tale, she had appeared and disappeared, leaving me back with the Yankees. On acid.

That trip was one of the strongest I have ever had. It lasted hours and hours. I swam out to the raft, climbing aboard while the trio dodged motor yachts, until finally stopping by a ferry-sized craft. Everyone came to life when they saw the permanently fixed smile on my face. I mean, I think of myself as a very easy person to get along with. Sometimes I think I'm a philosopher, but some describe me as a Thai hippie crossed with a Cockney hooligan! I guess I can understand it when people say I'm so deep I'm drowning; then again, I love constructive conversation and can talk about anything from the life of a plant to Tyson biting Holyfield's ear off. You either understand and relate to where I'm coming from or else you think I talk crap, but if you're reading this now I guess you're with me.

Anyway, at least one of the Harvard graduate friends thought I was one of the most interesting people they'd ever met. As the details of my fractured state of mind began to dawn on them, the Charlied-up angel girls begged me to tell them just what I'd been up to. While the crew in white uniforms set sail for open waters, out came the coke-y nose bag and the race was on again. Oh boy!

I couldn't keep the straw in a straight line, never mind focus on the powder. The girls sat me down and chopped up two huge runways on a mirror, holding the platform and straw to my hooter whilst I tried to become a hoover. My body stiffened as the tiny particles sizzled on my beleaguered brain. Most of the channels to my nerve centre were open due to the LSD, and I could feel every single granule sticking to the inside of my nose and brain. Pretty scary, I can tell ya. My eyes were almost popping out of my head as the cocaine closed all the open channels that the LSD had unlocked. Time was running out, and doors seemed to slam shut in my mind. But hang on, something was touching my lips . . .

The vision seemed to come from the back of my mind along a round, neon-lit metal tunnel until it reached the pupils in my eyes. In my stoned state I suddenly realised one of the girls was kissing me wildly and had her hand down the front of my shorts. I couldn't believe it! Suddenly she stopped, smiling, and suggested the three of us should play a game. I looked to my right as another babe stood topless on the table, performing some kind of erotic dance. The coke took over and I rose to my feet. There were only the three of us in the cabin, but much as I wanted to get involved, the paranoia was raging. I knew the guys on deck were heterosexual, but that wasn't enough for me to feel safe: I was completely off my nut and totally vulnerable with it.

Suppose they were bisexual – there was no way I could defend myself against four guys. Looking back, these entire thought processes seem ridiculous, but that's what coke and acid do to you. I was out of control. I wasn't me. I was some poor, frightened, confused animal who didn't just look a gift horse in the mouth, but tried to shoot it and sell it on as dog food.

I smashed a champagne bottle on the bar and warned the girls that if anyone came near me they'd get it. The girls were shocked and frightened – course they were! – and left the cabin screaming. Moments later all four guys came charging into the room. I grabbed a corkscrew and yelled to them, 'Stay back!'

They could easily have chinned me, and possibly should have, but instead they tried to calm me down.

'It's the drugs, mate. They're making you paranoid. You need to get some rest!'

Little of this logic crawled into my coke-shrunk mind. I told them all to move away from the door and let me out of the room. Suddenly, I made a break for the exit, running along the narrow corridor up some steps on to the deck. When I saw the sea it felt like a heart attack.

'Where *am I*?'

I screamed at the girls cowering at the back of the boat. Everyone was on deck now, trying to calm me down. They sensed this was totally out of character. Suddenly I freaked and launched myself into the sea, hitting the water with my stomach and sinking beneath the waves. My arms and legs were paralysed, but the guys had hold of me and weren't letting go. I felt myself being dragged back on to the yacht and then quietly passed out.

I awoke to find myself being gently shaken until my eyes opened and met the glaring stares of the friends around the bed. I felt groggy but otherwise more or less fine. They immediately clocked the change of character as my famous Chelsea beamer grinned from ear to ear. The girls told me what had happened and how I tried to escape by jumping ship. At first I didn't believe it, but eventually was forced to realise what I'd done. I was so embarrassed I couldn't apologise enough, especially to the beauties who'd tried to bed me. If I'd been in my right mind, I'd have jumped on them at the sign of a threesome!

The yacht pulled into Barcelona to re-stock provisions for a trip to the Caribbean. Everyone wanted me to go with them, but I was missing my girlfriend. The airport wasn't far from the harbour, so I thanked the American crew, swapping addresses and taking snapshots before making my way to a taxi rank. They all looked really sad when I had to go, which still amazes me. I waved goodbye, jumped into a taxi and sped off to the airport. Within hours I was back at Gatwick.

Thank fuck!

# 4 Beetle Juice

One thing I love just as much as partying is sleep. I adore my kip and have been known to go under for fourteen hours or more. One Saturday afternoon in '93, I'd spent a whole day trying to book a flight to Ibiza for the next day and wasn't happy at having to confirm an early morning flight. Still, I was jobless, free and determined to stay on the island for the whole summer. The one thing that made matters a bit awkward was not having a motor in England – I've always had cars and wasn't one for making conversations with cab drivers. What could I do?

Our family neighbours Mr & Mrs S.O. Dull had gone on holiday to France, leaving keys to the house in the trusty hands of my lovable mum. I knew they kept the keys to a car in the garage on a hook in the kitchen. Surely no one would notice the motor being gone a few hours? I desperately needed transport to London, cos I had to meet a pal who owed me 200 quid. Because of a crushing lack of funds, my options were severely limited. That was it, my mind was made up.

I zigzagged a route through the garden, sneaking through the back door like a cat burglar. The hung-up set of keys belonged to a Volkswagen, which confused me, because usually they drove a Volvo. A brown sheet covered a smallish vehicle in the garage. Like a child unwrapping Christmas presents, I ripped the sheet off to reveal a bright-green Beetle. The driver's door was unlocked but it wouldn't open. Shit! Luckily, the passenger side would, so I slipped into the hot seat. Tucked in the glove compartment was the holy scroll of the vehicle registration document. I memorised the name before checking the engine. At its best, German ingenuity is as hard to match as their football, especially those old-school engines. One turn of the key brought Herbie to life again, puffing and panting, until out came the distinctive purr of Beetles worldwide. I used the remote to open and close the garage door and was free to hit the road. Herbie Rides Again!

Once in east London I drove straight to a pub where several friends of mine had already been drinking for all of five hours. The lads were celebrating the release of another mate, Ian, fresh off a train after serving two years. I knew him myself from gang-fighting days, when his family lived in the rougher parts of London. His escape came through his father's successful furniture-removal business, which pulled in enough money in just a year to move the family further afield.

By closing time the guys were legless. Ian could really hold his drink and insisted that everyone went round to his place, 20 minutes away. Ian and another lad, Jason, jumped in the Beetle. We dashed through Bethnal Green and perhaps it wasn't so surprising when we attracted the attentions of a lawman. They must have followed us for all of ten minutes. Suddenly I took a right swing, turning down a quiet road and, amazingly, Dibble continued straight ahead without even glancing at us. There I was, sitting pissed with two ex-cons swigging from cans of beer and smoking hash, in a vehicle that was practically stolen! I couldn't help thinking about this, which made it even more difficult to drive and listen to directions.

As we reached the next junction two sets of headlights came screaming round the corner on both sides of the road. Immediately I slammed the brakes on, nearly sending my inebriated passengers hurtling through the windscreen and spraying warm beer everywhere.

Cars coming up fast from the rear left us totally blinded. Suddenly I could see silhouettes of men with guns, and within seconds the car was surrounded by policemen pointing automatic weapons at us. Shit, this was a big one.

A voice on a megaphone instructed the lads to raise their hands where they could be seen. Like a pride of lions, the pack moved in for the kill, screaming at me to unlock the door, which couldn't be opened even if I wanted it to.

'I can't! It won't open. It's jammed.'

The officers thought I was playing about and were getting more and more angry. For a split second I thought I was gonna be shot, as the SO19 team grappled with the door handle. They made Jason and Ian get out of the passenger door first, forcing them to kneel down with their hands together behind their heads.

The three officers pointing guns at me on the driver's side resembled Ninja warriors, except that instead of swords they had these shooters. It was hard to think of them as human beings, because these geezers with families and mums and brothers were highly trained and potential killers. Armed police were everywhere, with weapons poised. Once the boys were safely handcuffed, the squads moved in to search the car. I was virtually shitting myself, drunk as a skunk and with breath that could knock a person out.

Frightened, I pleaded with the plodder in charge that I'd just bought the car from the previous owner only days ago. I showed them the log book and explained I was just dropping my pals off before going home to sleep. Standing in the middle of a whole SO19 squad, I managed to ask what all the fuss was about, but didn't get an answer. Dibble was more interested in whether I had insurance. For some reason I told the truth and admitted that the vehicle wasn't insured for me to drive. Every radio in the vicinity came to life as the operators raised a coded alarm.

I was advised not to drive the motor and told that if I was spotted again that night I'd definitely be arrested. The crack police squad then jumped into their vehicles and sped into the night, leaving three drunken louts scratching their heads and giggling loudly. God only knows who or what they were looking for, but it was a lucky escape – they were after bigger fish than us. We checked the coast was clear and set off to Ian's gaff.

Shortly afterwards, shaken but not too stirred, I went straight home to pack my stuff, but on arrival I noticed a light on in the neighbours' house. My heart missed a succession of beats. Why do things have to happen in threes? First my pal only had a hundred quid, then we got stopped by SO19, and now I'm about to be caught bang to rights at the wheel of a stolen car!

I was sweating even more than when the Old Bill had me spreadeagled on the tarmac. This could cause a serious rift between both families. They might even want me nicked and ruin a five-year clean sheet! I had no option other than to face the music and try to front it, because time was running out and the flight to Ibiza took off in just four hours. Pulling into the driveway, I cautiously approached the front door and rang the bell. Minutes passed without any signs of life coming from the house. I put the key in the chamber and quietly opened the door, just wide enough to stick my head through. Nobody seemed to be home, so I returned the car to its garage.

Feeling confident enough, I went back home and marched into our kitchen to find Mr Dull having a chat with Dad. Oh no! They were locked in conversation and neither acknowledged me as I silently walked past to my bedroom. Half an hour later Dad was yelling.

'Wayne! Get down here.'

Oh creepers!

I thought I was done for, but amazingly Dad asked – and I kid you not – if I wanted the green VW Beetle that the neighbours kept in the garage! He explained that if I wanted it, the log book would have to be re-registered before I could drive it. Apparently the vehicle had belonged to an armed robber who was on the Most Wanted list. No wonder the Dib were all over us! Dad said he'd sort out the paperwork while I was away, so that when I returned everything would be legal. In a state of shock I finished packing, got a taxi to the airport and took flight to Ibiza.

# 5 Models Inc.

Carl Jung's *Synchronicity* plays a major role in my life and the lives of each living soul on this marvellous plant. The meaning of coincidence and the influence it has on our lives is pretty awesome. So when I find myself in certain situations I won't necessarily regard myself as lucky (although I do thank my guardian spirits). I acknowledge that this given moment was meant to happen for my own personal growth. I can get people doing stuff they've never had the front to attempt before, and I love to liberate partners from inhibition. Maybe I dream too much, but any and all of these claims can be firmly backed up by my lavish photo and home-video collection, although I don't like to show them to anyone and everyone. In my heyday my brief encounters included pop stars, actresses and well-known models. Every year, for one week in Ibiza, I'd run up the flag and almost lose control of my senses. But apart from a short break in the Balearics in '96, my drug-taking days are over. Why? Because cocaine finally started ruining my life.

Things have changed considerably since I first started taking drugs. Once, I seemed to be able to handle any amount of narcotics and still hold sensible conversations with friends or potential skirt. Not any more! Even as long ago as '96, coke was making me feel paranoid and introverted, although that year I stupidly had one last blast.

I arrived at Space on Sunday morning, fresh from an eight-hour kip. At first I promised myself I wouldn't take any drugs and, if anything, just get absolutely plastered on cheap booze. But it's a different matter to say that to yourself in a quiet moment at home than it is in the confines of a crowded party. Especially when you're virtually an addict and saying no to toot is like not eating would be for a normal person. The trouble with too much toot is you don't eat, either.

The terraces at Space were rammed with differing flamboyant characters, dancing anywhere they could. I entered the dark corridor to go for a sly leak, listening to the pounding techno, which seemed strangely incongruous so early on in the day. Standing at the nearest bar were three girls dressed like Goa hippies. They wore brightly printed Indian shirts, loose-fitting linen trousers, square-toed sandals and Buddhist bags across their shoulders. I was dressed pretty similarly, I guess, wearing hand-made baggy trousers from Thailand, a shirt from Tibet and sandals from Africa. A right walking flippin' geography lesson! As I passed by, they greeted me warmly, but I was so desperate for a piss I had to apologise and quickly disappeared into the stone-cold lavatory.

A security guard stood in the space between the men's and women's, making sure the two didn't mix. His job was also to make sure no one sniffed lines or had any form of sex in the cubicle. You don't know if you're being watched from above or whether the doors are about to come crashing down.

As I relieved myself, an old Spanish woman came and cleaned the floor around me. Perturbed, I went outside, but the hippie girls had gone. I looked around and could see them dirty dancing. Our eyes met and we all started laughing. I nodded and headed back outside, but I couldn't help thinking how familiar one of them looked. I'd just about reached the light of day when I heard a female voice behind me.

'Hello. My name is Nina.'

She sounded foreign and sexy.

'My friend Alexandria would like to buy you a drink.'

I wasted no time and in an instant was with the girls, gyrating and giggling on the dance floor. They didn't want to go outside on to the terrace and instead lurked by the bar, where a brain-pulverising succession of tequila slammers left us more than merry. As closing time was rapidly approaching, I invited them back to the villa, where a party was already under way. Most wanted to go home, though, and I was left with Alexandria. It could have been worse!

I'd promised my friends I'd bring back a load more gear for

them. We were staying in a rented mansion up in the hills, which belonged to a famous actor. On the way to San Antonio, Alexandria confessed to being a 'household name' in the modelling industry and she told me that, if she went back to my place, I'd have to promise to behave because she was a decent girl and preferred to get to know me first (or at least wait until the second date!). She asked to be alone with me at the villa, so she could learn more about me. She wasn't your average girl, although I must admit I listened to what she said about being a household name and didn't take much notice. (I'm not easily impressed.)

At the Café del Mar we bumped into Sid, who was scoring everything in sight. Quietly we made our way up to the hills. The journey should have taken about 45 minutes at the present controlled rate of acceleration, but the Charlie was burning holes in my pocket.

'Mind if I have a line?' I asked.

Alexandria said she didn't want any, but lined them up for me all the same, which was a bit like lining up a load of ears in front of Mike 'Chomp Chomp' Tyson.

I just couldn't help myself.

By the time we reached the villa I'd caned a gram and was just starting to quieten down. To tell the truth, I was mortified. I could even feel the change of character coming over me as the toot invaded my battered mind. The worst thing was, Alexandria noticed too.

We came to the enormous (mad)house and went straight upstairs, where I left Alex, insisting I wouldn't be long. Downstairs, the whole gang was pilled up and acting really crazy. The girls were wearing nothing but G-strings and were crawling on all fours across a long mahogany table. Not to be left out, the lads were pouring bottles of champagne over the lasses' nubile, tanned bodies, while the girls just laughed and lapped up the attention. Quietly I emptied the contents of several small plastic bags on to a smaller glass table and everyone – me included – dug in, finishing the entire stash of Chas within the hour.

While I sat upright in a semi-stupor, one of the girls told me she recognised Alexandria's face from a recent cover of *Vogue* and that she was 'tipped to become a supermodel'. Now normally this is the sort of information I'd take with an enormous pinch of salt (and, why not, another sniff of Charlie), but this time it was different. Worryingly, I too felt I knew her face from somewhere. What if she really was a rising model? Look at the state of me! I did know Alex's face from somewhere, I just couldn't place it. I was having trouble speaking anyway, and the thought of her being famous shattered whatever fragile self-confidence I had left. Suddenly everything fell into place, with me – I'm ashamed to admit it – totally off my face!

After another hour the girls downstairs started moaning about me leaving Alexandria alone in her room. The nosebag took hold, though, and I was riveted to the seat. Eventually Alex came down and asked to be taken home. It turned out she'd fallen asleep and woken up to find herself still solo. And she was far from pleased.

The entire journey back to her apartment was in deathly silence. The more I thought about saying anything, the more paranoid and awkward I felt about it, and in any case sensible sentences disappeared from my mind like brain cells. There was no point in saying, 'I'm not usually like this', because she'd never give me another opportunity. She felt that I'd been disrespectful and she was right. Finally she warned me not to speak to her again.

As the car arrived at her apartment she jumped out, slammed the door and waltzed out of my life. There I was: in Ibiza, caned to the gills on Charlie, living it up in a film star's mansion, with a supermodel in my bedroom, and I still – still! – managed to fuck it up. I saw Alexandria again – but only smirking at me from the pages of a million magazines. She was gooorgeous . . .

Drugs really can suck, man!

# 6 Forest's Story – The End of Innocence

This chapter contains some very sensitive information. Let's just say: I was told this story by Chris . . .

Forest hated summertime. It seemed everyone in town apart from him flew off to Spain somewhere. He'd never been abroad before, spending most of his time working on his parents' remote farm. As a child, he'd been inseparable from his mother, always by her side wherever she went and not allowed to speak or mix with other children. A lot of the other kids felt sorry for the introverted lad, blaming his reclusive personality on the domineering bloodline around him. Even in the playground at break times he'd sit alone, not saying a word to a soul. The other kids were beyond trying to get him to join in their games – they'd passed that stage years ago. He was a loner, and that was that.

It wasn't that much different in his adult years. He was still glued to his mum. The only reason he wasn't a virgin was because a distant cousin from America had forced the shy lad to have sex with a prostitute, on his last drunken visit to England. That was over five years ago. Secretly Forest really enjoyed the bunk up, but at the time he was scared stiff!

The family business seemed forever in debt, which meant work, work and more work. Now 30, Forest yearned for closeness, but the nearest he'd got to a friendship was with Ricky, who'd always tried to speak to Forest and get him involved with whatever the rest of the group was doing. The previous year Ricky asked him if he'd like to go on holiday to Ibiza with ten others. No one else wanted Forest to go, but Ricky was the leader of the pack, and what he said was final. Forest wasn't really sure why someone as popular as Ricky paid him any attention, but there you go. After seeing him around since childhood, Forest regarded the much-travelled lad as a pal . . . sort of.

Only a few weeks before, Ricky had again mentioned Ibiza to the farmer, who'd thought about it since. Eventually he set out to ask Ricky if the offer still stood. It was hard for Forest to walk into a packed bar and announce his urge to break free from the ball and chain around his leg, but somehow he was determined to go through with it, even if everyone laughed, sending him deeper into the realms of seclusion. This was a last desperate attempt to ditch the life he'd grown to loathe.

With heart in mouth, he entered the bar, walking straight up to Ricky, who was both surprised and glad to see Forest out and about without his mum. Although the pair had never had a conversation past three minutes, the respect was mutual. After short deliberation, Ricky was happy to bring the loner on board.

'It's a great idea. You're more than welcome,' he chirped. 'We're leaving tomorrow night, so if I were you I'd get on the phone and book a ticket sharpish.'

Forest literally jumped for joy. Ricky told his pals he was a closet party animal waiting to escape. But he took the farmer to one side and declared, 'Look, Forest, I know you've lived a sheltered life, mate, but before you decide to come with us, you have to know that when we're in Ibiza we take a lot of drugs. Some of the boys even sell drugs. I don't want you to get the wrong idea, mate. We're not a bunch of innocent school kids going on summer holiday. I know you've never been away before, but I can't promise your safety. Ibiza's one of the most insane party islands we've ever been to . . . Just so long as you understand what I'm saying, I don't mind you coming along.'

Before leaving Forest agreed, feeling really good about himself and the immediate change that had transpired. The weight of the entire world was suddenly lifted from his tiny shoulders. It was only a week's holiday, but if felt like the start of a new life. If he was gonna be a loner anyway, he might as well be one who travelled.

Leaping the first hurdle, with only two more to jump, he wondered how to tell his mother. She certainly wouldn't be happy about the seemingly spontaneous decision he'd already made. Luckily, the money he'd saved over the last ten years could cover the holiday costs ... He didn't need to ask for readies.

When it came, the reaction from his mother was much more severe than he'd expected. She told him that if he left there would be no home for him when he returned! All his life he'd done everything to please her, without ever once answering back, or disobeying her. His life was not his own. And yet, something buried deep inside him manipulated his normal thought processes and he acted defiantly out of character. He was going ... and that was that.

There was no shortage of flights, so he booked one for early the next morning, then returned home and packed. Neither of his parents spoke to him as he rushed about the house getting his stuff; but not wanting to leave on such bad terms, he tried telling them how much this trip meant to him. His unconditional love for the people who brought him into this world had never been in question. Whilst the other youngsters in the village were discovering puberty and the difference between males and females, Forest was mucking out cowsheds and seeing that the cattle, pigs, sheep and chickens got fed regularly. He'd been doing that for as long as he remembered and never once turned his back on the responsibility. Unmoved by his speech, the wall of silence strengthened.

Forest was very emotional, and something intuitively told him that this would indeed be the last time he'd see his parents. He was only going away for seven days and seven nights, no big deal, but this was a last goodbye. Feeling shunned and dejected, the time came for him to go outside and wait for Ricky. He finally left the hostile parents he loved so much sleeping in front of the TV and, like a soldier off to battle, slowly walked along the driveway up to the junction to meet his new-found buddies.

An hour passed with no sign of the group, and Forest sitting on his case fearing the worse. What to do now? Suddenly he heard music and saw headlights fast approaching. The Range Rover pulled up.

'Sorry, mate. Bung yer gear in the back and hop in. We're running a bit late.'

Ricky began the frenetic dash to the airport.

'You've never taken drugs before, have ya, Forest?' queried the driver. 'What about alcohol? You ever had a drink?'

Forest hadn't – he didn't like the smell.

As he answered, Ricky reached into his pocket and pulled out a tiny wrap. He opened the square piece of paper and put a card into the white powder.

'Here, put this on the back of your hand and sniff it up your nose.'

Ricky loaded both his nostrils.

'Right, Forest. This is your last chance to back out.'

'I'm ready. Let's do it.'

'OK,' said Ricky. 'We got our passports, tickets, luggage, a full tank of gas, packet of fags, it's dark, we're wearing sunglasses [handing Forest a spare set of bins] and about to go on a most unprecedented adventure! Hit it!'

The Range Rover went from 0 to 60 in seconds as Forest's mind exploded. Forest leaned across and put his hand firmly on the car horn. The duo drove to the airport at top speed all the way. Forest was feeling a different person already: this drive on the wild side was definitely therapeutic.

Once in the terminal they met up with the clan, who welcomed their new travelling companion. Ricky asked Forest to carry one of his bags, because he couldn't manage. Hours later the entourage pulled into their rented villa, by which time Forest was slightly bladdered from duty-free drinks on the plane. A scramble for the best bedrooms left three people in the swimming pool fully clothed with all their cases. Ricky took the bag he'd given his room-mate to hold.

Stuffing his hand into the canvas holdall, he pulled out a big bag of white powder and another packed with white tablets. Greek Chris barged into the room and said he'd be outside in the car. Forest had seen him in town on numerous occasions; in fact, so had everybody else. The getaway driver drove 100 m.p.h. everywhere he went, with girls holding on for dear life and music you could hear fields away.

Immediately, Ricky asked if Forest wanted to go for a drive. En route, Forest admired the scenery. The mountains against the night sky were looking awesome. Ricky nervously announced the Guardia Civil were following them, before slipping the two bags to Forest in the back.

'Shall I put my foot down or what?' the driver asked.

'Do what you gotta, mate, but get us the fuck out of here.'

The driver slowed down as if to stop by the roadside, allowing the jeep to pull up behind them. But as the soldiers scrambled from their vehicle towards the car, Chris slammed his foot on the gas and they shot off out of there. Forest thought he heard shots fired but didn't dare turn round to check, and was oblivious to the danger. He was just completely excited, and flying on the adrenaline rush.

The runaway vehicle touched 120 m.p.h. on a long straight road, but suddenly, out of nowhere, there were two waiting jeeps blocking their path. There was no way the motor would stop in time. If they swerved to miss, their car would crash into the rocks at the roadside. With nowhere else to go, the car smashed through the roadblock, veering out of control across a car park and through the front window of a supermarket. The sound of breaking glass was excruciating, but Forest couldn't move a muscle. He tried opening his eyes, but the lids wouldn't budge. Strangely enough, his hearing seemed more acute, and there were sirens ringing out. He remembered thinking about getting to a bomb shelter, before an eerie silence prevailed. Before long, voices penetrated the dark environment he was trapped in, until he realised they spoke in Spanish.

Suddenly, a perfect English-speaking voice called his name.

'Hello, Forest. Forest, can you hear me?'

He murmured that he could.

'Open your eyes, Forest, I need to speak with you. I'm from the British Embassy.'

The blinding light stung his eyes like petrol. He wanted to cover them with his hands, but the pain was unbearable. Looking round the faces staring down at him, he knew his nightmare was no dream. He was lying in a hospital bed. Soon enough he asked the smartly dressed gentleman where his friends were.

'I'm afraid I have bad news,' came the reply. 'Do you feel strong enough to hear it?'

Forest gasped.

'What's happened?'

'You've been in a coma for three weeks, after the crash you were involved in. Do you remember the crash, Forest?'

He thought so. But where was Ricky?

'Sorry to tell you, Forest, but Ricky didn't make it. The driver, Chris, wasn't badly injured. He's already been taken to a prison on the mainland because drugs were found in the vehicle.'

'What do you mean, "He didn't make it"?' gasped Forest. 'Are you saying he's dead?'

He was and, worse, they'd found a substantial amount of drugs in the vehicle.

'Do you know anything about this?' asked the man from the embassy.

'I think so.'

As Forest started to take in everything that was happening to him, the man explained that the police wanted to know who the bags belonged to. It turned out that Chris had told them the drugs were Ricky's.

'The law prohibits me from giving you legal advice,' continued the man, 'but I will contact a good lawyer for you. The case will go to trial and I've no doubt a substantial amount of money will have to be paid up front, if you're granted bail. You'll probably be restricted to the Spanish mainland. You with me so far?'

Forest couldn't believe it.

'No, this can't be happening! Where are my friends? You're trying to trick me.'

'Stay calm, Forest, the Guardia will be along any minute now,' insisted the embassy envoy. 'They're going to take you to the station and then to a prison hospital unit in Barcelona. You've never been in trouble before, so that should help your case. Apparently it's the first time you've been abroad. With a bit of luck, a court will hear the case within the next couple of weeks, but be warned: it could take months.'

Forest was dumbfounded. He had something of a panic attack.

'Please don't let them take me away. I can't handle it!'

He began screaming.

'I'm afraid the best I can do is put you in touch with some English-speaking lawyers and give someone a message in England on your behalf. It's probable that you'll be sharing cells with Chris. He's been away before. It's not as bad as people think. Here comes your escort now; they speak no English, mostly sign language. It's good that you learn quickly – these guys aren't like British bobbies.'

Forest was distraught.

They started to dress him and get him ready to go. He was in pain, both internally and externally: his battered, bruised body hadn't been exercised for weeks. Like a tin man in urgent need of oil, he began putting his ripped clothes on. The Guardia took him to a waiting jeep downstairs and off towards the secure medical wing. The lad had never even spoken to a policeman, much less got a full blazing escort to a prison in Europe. Sadness passed the time until they entered the prison's huge gates, Forest's resting place for the following three months.

The two bags had Forest's dabs all over them. He was charged with possession and intent to supply and import a controlled drug. One bag contained 1,500 Es, the other an ounce of sniff. Chris was charged with attempted murder and got five years, whilst Forest got seven in one of Spain's most notorious prisons. Almost ten years later he was spotted at a full-moon party in Thailand, weighing in at sixteen stone, with multicoloured dreadlocks to his waist. He was covered from head to foot in yellow paint, with a huge tattoo that read simply 'Forest' across his chest.

It could have been worse.

It could have been 'Hello, Mum.'

# **7** Cocaine Madness

The long bony finger of fate comes in many guises. No 20th century individual could even begin to understand the thinking of the right side of the human brain. It's this section where the real power of the mind is located, a home to destiny and all things magical, with few able to predict where its quirks or characteristic would lead to next. Nor do we know the source responsible for pushing those buttons, or synchronising such elements so that each moment tastes like perfection. It's a funny old cabbage, the brain, when you get to thinking about it. Which is something I do often, as you may be starting to gather.

One day back in '94, I felt like I was having a real day of reckoning. It's a place where many of us have been or end up going to at some point in our drug-consuming careers. A dead end. An impasse. Sometimes, a final dance with the devil. Do we have a choice about whether we want to go there? Do we fuck ... How can we under the influences of mind-altering substances? We're not kidding anybody, so let's all stop pretending.

In 1994, out of a thousand people happily dancing in a club called Kaos, in Port San Antonio, I was about to face an unexpected test. Simply, I was about to enter the Twilight Zone. It all started with a series of involuntary limb movements – and then 'Wayne Anthony of London, come on down!'

I glanced around the club to check if anyone was noticing my suddenly violent new dance moves. Although I didn't know it, your hardcore party animal had already stepped off the face of real time into the realms of a cocaine-induced tunnel reality. I was adrift in the terrible mental netherworlds that exist between pain and pleasure. I was lost within my own psychotic world, unaffected externally by the chaotic scenes of clubland going off around me. I slipped quietly out of the building, and struggled to deal with the madness.

Somehow I managed to find a taxi, but other than repeating my address several times to the driver, not a word was said on the 20-minute journey. I cautiously walked through the villa's wooden gates and conducted a quick perimeter search. Only when I was absolutely sure that the coast was clear did I lift a rock in the flower bed to pick up a bunch of keys. The Spanish house was fitted with metal shutters, covering all points of entry to the building. Each window and door had its own motor and could be opened separately, if required, one flick of the switch slowly opening all the shutters. There was only one remote control for the lot of them, so after much deliberation it had been agreed that the plastic remote and keys should be left in the general vicinity of the house.

The metal grinding sound of the battery-operated motors caused me to flinch nervously, whilst grinding my teeth into blunt boulders. Keeping a sharp look-out for anyone trying to sneak up on me, I tiptoed across the garden and in through the back door. I'd been drinking heavily, so I had to visit the toilet at regular intervals, but each time I arrived my bladder started to malfunction. It gave me real stick, playing havoc with my waterworks and at times even causing pain. A thimble of urine could take up to 20 minutes ... Talk about taking the piss. Then there was the defecation, but I won't get into that.

To encourage the tiny water supply to shred its drops, I'd gyrate my hips or pace the bathroom, hoping to work the water. I'd always described my drug use as recreational and moderate – certainly not like the big-time hoovers I often hung out with. Then again, not being short of a few quid separated me from your average user, who might spend a nifty per day on the stuff. In one session I had been known to blow a grand's worth of trumpet up my noble hooter.

Seeing as I was only really caning it once or twice a week, I was fairly content that I didn't have a problem. Then again, I'd regularly condemn as addicts people who sniffed every day, even though they might have done less than half of what I'd do in a month.

I emptied the contents of a bag I'd bought earlier on to a slab of marble. I was starting to have huge regrets about taking the drug to begin with. It was quite confusing really: when I didn't take the drug, I tended to think of the crystallite flakes burning through my hooter. On the other hand, when I did it, I always ended up cursing myself for having no willpower. I stuck my head into the pile of powder and inhaled. Charlie hadn't crossed my mind for most of the night until I'd become bored and got involved. I felt bitterly disappointed, though, let down by this pathetic craving for a drug that had totally lost its appeal to me. But it was too late. Like a child running wild around a toy shop, I'd ventured out of my way to sniff as much gear as I could buy. The class-A drug had achieved its objective: this unhappy clapper was now locked into total body consciousness.

I was aware of every movement I made, from the thought process itself through to the responding action. I felt as if I could practically tune into each living organ, including the thunderous sound of my palpitating heartbeat merging with blood passing along the main arteries, and the pulse connecting each vein.

Not knowing what to do with myself, I stood motionless in the middle of the living room, staring into space. The villa was stocked with all the mod cons, including a stereo, video, three different computer games-consoles and a TV, which flickered quietly in the background. Suddenly, something splashing in the swimming pool brought me sharply back to life and I shot outside to investigate. One of the garden statues was at the bottom of the water.

Scanning the area, I rushed back inside and activated the main security shutters. Like a war bunker set in mountain rock, the windows and doors locked into place. No one could come in and I certainly wasn't in the mood for getting out. The entire villa was now watertight: nothing less than the fire department could penetrate the steel barriers.

I sat down to play Tomb Raider on the games console but couldn't concentrate for more than three minutes at a time. Although I'd seen tougher days, this was a bad one. The wired wool, the caned unable! The palms of my hands were so sweaty

## Spanish Highs

I had trouble keeping the spliff dry. I blew tons of grunge from my nose, with more to follow. The silence of the house and a fervid buzz stopped me from flushing the toilet too often, and the bowl, filled to the brink, was at breaking point before I decided to pull the chain and liberate two hours' contents. The bog roll was too much for the European-size toilet and the water began to rise, until it spilt out on to the bathroom floor, soaking everything. Ohhh . . . SHIT!

I was helpless to stop the pongy flood, and so stood there panicking whilst the water level on the ground got higher and flowed out under the door, out to the, er, back passage. Attempting to ride the rapids, I yanked the shower curtain down and tried blocking the bowl, without much luck. Where the fuck was the water main?

Amazingly, as quickly as it had begun, the flow ceased. My body temperature continued to rise: my war bunker had become my tomb. I prayed for Lara Croft to come crashing through the wall and rescue me, but knew that this was hopeless as she wouldn't stand the smell. Gasping for oxygen, I didn't even think of opening the shutters for fresh air, or to check whether my friends had returned home. Instead I went into the kitchen and stuck my head by the freezer, not giving the waterlogged bathroom and passage a second thought. Time went by before eventually I decided I should clean the place up. The mop wasn't getting me anywhere, so I grabbed the laundry and covered the floor in T-shirts, jeans, towels, shorts and bed-sheets. Then I practically collapsed, but getting any sleep was about as likely as the *Daily Sport* running an issue without any shagging in it, cos of the coke. That's me, you understand, not the newspaper!

Every second dragged out for an hour as I tried to enter a meditation mode of relaxation. The buzzing of a mosquito flying past my face drew my attention, but couldn't force a response. My mind spun with negative flashbacks from years ago. I was shot, out of it and insecure. It felt like my entire human mind and body were about to start breaking down. I'd reached this horrible point after eighteen strenuous hours of party mania. Thoroughly exhausted, I laid on the sofa wishing, hoping and praying for some kip, but instead went into rapid eye movement. If my eyes opened for any reason, it felt like the cycle had to be started again. This was true hell.

A stinging sensation on my cheekbone automatically brought my hand slapping into my face. The kamikaze mosquito evaded being splattered and landed on a cushion. I decided to let the insect live and maintain the current mellow flow, cos in this state the last thing I needed was any more bad karma. But this was not to be. Two bites on my legs brought the rolled-up magazine . . . Swat!

I listened for sounds of the approaching enemy. The buzzing of kamikazes in attack formation came towards me, criss-crossing my body at all angles. Moments later, there was silence once more, not a buzz except my own, chemically induced psychosis. I began a random search of the room, looking for tiny dark spots on the whitewashed walls. An hour passed and I was still a Jedi Knight in hot pursuit of an enemy unit. Inspired by Obi Wan Kenobi, I homed in on the flutter of micro-wings and my purpose-made sabre brought immediate death to the insect. The excitement was too much. I let out a loud Indian war cry (at least that's how it sounded to me!) and I danced around the coffee table, chanting and singing. I was a chief hunter and warrior.

My senses were heightened by the quiver and the adrenaline rush of locating the mosquito and squashing it into the pristine paintwork. The ram raiders blatantly landed on various parts of my body and didn't give a fuck if I saw them. For each one I flattened, a loud cheer rang throughout the villa. I was having trouble containing my emotions and was ecstatic every time I put one's lights out. With the imaginary sound of tribal drums pounding in the background, a smell of fresh blood and the wind of the fan blowing gave the hunt an outdoor, cinematic effect. The assault on Precinct Thirteen raged on relentlessly for another hour before I finally felt relaxed again, whereupon I realised that I was slowly going mad.

They were still biting me, despite being attacked by insect spray. The aggravated itching from earlier chomps was driving me bananas. I developed a bizarre, avant-garde nervous twitch, reminiscent of the religious rituals of the post-Crimean period, or Roger Moore's eyebrows. Each time something gently brushed my skin, it sent me into spasms and then I'd miss the target.

A long wait was finally rewarded and at last I'd murdered what was left in the room, and settled down to sleep. It didn't last. A thousand different thoughts entered my head for careful consideration, as I burst into tears for no apparent reason. Angry at myself for not being able to regain control over my thoughts and emotions, I urgently needed help but couldn't cry out for it. For the first time in 29 years, I actually thought I was about to permanently lose my marbles.

In a desperate attempt to save my sanity, I telephoned a friend in England for advice on insomnia. Stretch should have sorted me out: he'd been doing drugs since the year dot. If he couldn't submit several remedies then no one could. But considering the villa wasn't stocked with any (legal!) pharmaceuticals or old wives' concoctions, he had a major challenge to overcome at four in the morning.

The phone rang for a while before a tired Stretch yelled down the receiver. In a frightened tone I begged for help from my mate, hundreds of miles away. But I had to do something to bring myself down.

On the advice of my sympathetic pal, I frantically searched the villa and discovered half a bottle of very strong cough mixture and a quarter-bottle of Jack Daniel's, which was immediately knocked back. Sanity beckoned, but I was already doing 90 in the opposite direction. I settled down on the couch and tuned into a German channel showing pictures of the earth taken via satellite, listening to some ambient chill-out . . . bollocks playing in the background! My heart rate had slowed, although I still felt wide awake. The lighting was off and the glimmer of candles lit the spacious room like miniature explosions. Something moving beneath the TV stand caught my attention. The shadows cast by the wooden unit made it difficult to see properly, but I was sure I saw the oversized legs of a spider. I firmly fixed my glare on the shadow as it ran across the floor and under the couch I lay on. I sprang into action, touching the floor but once, before leaping out into the passage and running into the bedroom for a baseball bat. Twenty minutes passed with me standing on the bed, weapon in hand poised for Valhalla.

The spider was far bigger than anything I'd seen in the *National Geographic* or Discovery Channel. This was Godzilla meets King Kong in *The Land That Time Forgot*. In short, it was my worst nightmare, and your poor maniac would need the front of Tesco's medicine cabinet to get out of this one.

I crept into the passage, preparing to meet the uncanny horror that lay in wait. Nothing out of the ordinary so far ... I made it into the kitchen and became fully armed with various kitchen knives sticking out of my belt. The couch stuck out like a virgin in a brothel, as if a spotlight marked the danger spot. Sweat streamed down my face, stinging both eyes, as a voice kept saying, 'Get the fuck out of there.' My fears gained momentum by the second.

Running into the room, I kicked the couch before retreating to the doorway. Nothing happened, so I did it again: this time I didn't run but stood to face the beast. Apart from hearing my heart racing at high speed, the room was silent and still. I flipped over the sofa, only to find an empty space, and began laughing out loud. Now a little more confident, I searched the whole villa and eagerly awaited the eight-legged fiend. Part of me was relieved not to find ze monsta, whilst the cocaine devil in me wanted to rip the beast to shreds and feed it to the neighbours' dogs. But was my imagination playing games with my senses?

There's no spider, man! I thought.

I suddenly felt ridiculous, and was glad I was alone. I dived back on to the couch and flicked through the satellite channels, to find nothing of interest showing. Suddenly, submerged in deep thought, I saw something move at the corner of my eye. When I faced the TV, I saw big, hairy spider's legs under the stand once more ... Except that this time there were loads of them. Suddenly the legs were carrying the TV across the floor.

I screamed loudly, falling over myself as I escaped the onslaught of spiders running riot. The bedroom door rocked the building's foundations as I slammed it shut behind me. A chest of drawers and a king-sized bed were barricaded against the door. I was trapped in the tiny square space, unable to reach the remote control for the automated shutters. But at least I was safe. Wasn't I?

The entire room seemed to breathe, making it bigger and smaller as it moved. The air supply fell dramatically and I gasped for fresh air as I underwent the early stages of my first ever total panic attack. The best I could do was wait hopefully for my friends to realise something must be wrong and raise the alarm, although they had no way of getting into the building. They'd probably think I took the keys in a drunken state and shacked up with a babe somewhere; in which case everyone would stay with friends until I raised my ugly head again. Very little sleeping was done in the villa because the whole group were party animals. God knows when I would be rescued from the waking nightmare's terrible clutches. For that matter, how was I to know if the whole globe had been invaded by the eight-legged critters?

I was plunged into self-loathing, and horror, and pondered the reality of not seeing the outside world again. What if a spider invasion had taken place? What if I was the only person left alive? What would I do? Where would I go? I had so little time, with so much more I wanted to see and to achieve. Why had it gone so wrong for me?

Why did I take drugs?

Why didn't I remind my family I loved them before flying to Ibiza?

Why had I not spoken to my closest friend for over five years, because of a minor dispute?

Why did I drive the woman I loved away?

And, mostly, why couldn't I have been someone else and not collapsed into this hedonistic lifestyle?

Was I crazy? Had I finally lost the plot?

My mind alive with thought, I was interrupted by the sound of the metal shutter raising outside the window. I screamed out of the window and one of the girls came charging round the corner. I quickly expressed my state of mind and pleaded for help from my friends, begging them not to let anyone take me to hospital. I dismantled the barricade, to be met head-on by the fuming Spanish landlord, who was none too pleased to find the villa in a real mess. Soaked dirty laundry littered the passageway, and I'd done some very peculiar furniture re-shufflements.

My friends somehow managed to convince the owner not to call the police, telling him that their pal was having a nervous breakdown. They gave him a hundred quid and off he went, leaving Buzz Lightyear and the crew to straighten the fiasco out. It only took ten minutes before I could feel myself returning to normal . . . or as normal as I could get. Apparently the cough mixture I'd swallowed was strong enough to have killed me, and I was lucky not to have necked the entire bottle. Fortunately I did make a full recovery and, apart from a smoke, I was too frightened to take hard drugs again that holiday.

The only visible scars left by my dance with the devil were a slight twitch in the shoulder, where I couldn't keep still for fear of being bitten by mosquitoes. The last time I gave in to the urge of sniffing a line, it took me right back to the tunnelled reality of that terrible experience, and left me with a permanent feeling of being close to the edge.

That day, I'd entered the real-time world of Never Never Land: a place inside our heads of equilibrium between sanity and genius, right and wrong, good and evil, happiness and sadness. The irony of it all being: I've recently been accused of promoting drugs!

# **8** Poster Wars

Puffs of smoke came out of my ears as I ranted and raged at the workers who'd sworn blind they plastered the club's posters around the island. I might occasionally be called a promoter, but this was one team I wouldn't be catapulting to the top division. If they couldn't or wouldn't be arsed to cut it, they were out.

Fly-posting is always the most important feature of any promotional campaign. In Ibiza, the days were long gone when clubs could rely on employees handing flyers directly to punters outside the gaff. The law had prohibited this form of 'harassment' and firmly established new guidelines for nightclub owners, with hefty fines following a legal slap on the wrist for anybody caught breaking the rules. But I was pissed off big time and getting more irate by the minute. As well as being unsure whether my own workers had really been putting the posters where they were meant to be, a bigger problem was that someone else had been ripping down my brightly coloured works of art and replacing them with their own bodged-up posters. This sent me through the roof. This was my big comeback – the big potato, the enormous aubergine. There was no way I was gonna let my return to the ring be spoiled by some blundering southpaw dodger.

I instructed workers in return to plaster over every 'Angel' poster on the island, then leapt into the motor, heading for the other promoter's villa. Once there, I confess to making a number of threats against any of his workers caught even touching my 'Love It' posters, never mind ripping the creations down. But unsurprisingly, the rival management team denied all knowledge of their team's ungentlemanly conduct and promised to investigate the claims. I wasn't convinced, but had to defer – for now.

The thing was: both organisations had come to Ibiza in the hope of having a profitable holiday and reinforcing their dance-scene street credibility. If you've read *Class of '88*, you'll be only too familiar – as I was – with the dubious, underhand tactics that promoters are well versed in, to drive their rivals out of town. There are more dirty tricks here than in the entire Arsenal midfield: we're looking at flyers being taken out of bars; posters being covered over or ripped down; fights on club-nights; and all kinds of other bollocks, not to mention the heavy stuff involving billiard balls in socks, and camping blades.

The 'Angel' promoters were new to Ibiza and I got the feeling they hadn't really got to grips with what the island was about. In fact, they had a skewed, Johnny Tourist view of Ibizan night-life, fuelled by hype and misinformation back in the UK. Every day they'd get completely off their nuts without doing any work, then expect their club nights to be successful. When no one turned up at the club, the workers got blamed for not pushing it hard enough. I heard some sad, but familiar reports. Tempers would flare daily, and the partners seemed to be fighting almost as much as they were partying. Now I may not be averse to the odd good time, but I've always gone out of my way to ensure that my parties are very professionally presented, meticulously organised and put together by firms of old-school promoters who've been around the block. If you weren't clued in, our friendly attitude to workers and other promoters could easily be mistaken for weakness, but that was certainly not the case. We were just a happy bunch, keeping ourselves to ourselves and making sure we didn't get dragged into the dispiriting office politics of English promoters who were abroad all season. My view is that there's no point in fighting – it solves nothing and projects bad karma to the punters. Then again, if someone does fuck you over, it's time to drop one on them . . . And we are not talking about a handshake.

Regrettably, the time had come to retaliate and show the 'Angel' lot just what was what. The dangers were paramount: something as seemingly petty as this could be the start of nasty peer-group rivalry, which could easily escalate into full-scale promoter war. The thing was, our respective weekly club events weren't even on the same night, so I couldn't help feeling that we'd been singled out as some kind of soft touch. That would never do.

I assured the shocked 'Angel' promoters of my prompt return, pending the future actions of their staff, then left for home. An emergency meeting was called at which my entire team were told to be extra-vigilant and report directly to me anyone seen tearing down or covering up posters. It's not that I'm paranoid (much), just vigilant, so I paid four different people decent wages to drive around checking the sites every day for two full weeks. The funny thing was: even before paying out the money, sadly I knew the outcome.

The call came early one morning. Some Spanish teenagers had been seen systematically destroying our posters without a care in the world. They weren't even trying to hide what they were doing. But instead of apprehending the suspects, I told my workers to follow the vandals and find out where they lived. For more than three hours the youths drove to each plot, before stopping outside the 'Angel' villa. Within 20 minutes I and a four-strong crew were in transit, after them.

The teenagers left before we even reached the door. Knuckles flew as we stormed on to the patio, where the moody promoters were counting complimentary club tickets. Only the company directors were taken from the villa, whilst the remaining occupants were warned that if we kidnappers were reported to the police, each of them would share the same, nicely grisly fate. The high altitudes meant much cooler temperatures, and after being taken up to the mountains and beaten black and blue, the four partners were left to walk home completely naked. Don't get me wrong here. I am a nice man. But they had taken the piss, especially and more so after being already warned about it. Terrified of staying on the island a day longer, the promoters decided to leave Ibiza pronto and perhaps try their luck next year. As far as I was concerned, our trouble was over. But I would always be wary.

On the morning of 'Love It's club night, a Guardia Civil jeep was parked outside our villa for a couple of hours. The villa was practically spotless, because our lads expected a visit from Dibble anyway (they, too, were not averse to the odd dirty trick). Everybody flushed their last bits of gear down the bog and sat peering through the wooden blinds. Two officers appeared from the villa opposite, got in the jeep and then sped off, leaving everybody in our crew massively disappointed that they'd panicked and lost their stashes.

Later that evening, a group from the PR team came to the villa in full fancy-dress costumes. Euro-Singo came dressed as Dracula with a red leopard-style haircut, Joanna resembled Morticia from the Addams family, whilst Jen looked like an exotic Indian dancer. Sally was a reasonable Sporty Spice, and I like to think I was a convincing Man in Black! It was left to Thomo to quickly change into a Gothic monk's outfit with a huge silver cross and chain dangling from his neck. We looked awesome – if, I must admit, completely bollockin' preposterous!

A meeting with the rest of the workers was arranged at a restaurant in Ibiza Town, but before we could do that, there was a quick pit-stop at Mambo to hand out complimentary passes to everyone we wanted to meet later. After a few rounds of chapitos we dived into the Vauxhall Corsa and shot along the one-way road for a couple of hundred yards, until we were abruptly stopped by two Guardia Civil soldiers jumping out into the road. Our crew of six was ordered out of the motor while one of the Dibbles searched the car, and another group of officers searched me and driver Thomo. Soon enough they were making us empty the contents of our pockets on to the bonnet of the car. Thomo had already slipped an eighth of sniff into his Calvin's, but hadn't had the time to hide the disco dust. I warily put my stuff on the bonnet, leaving the lump of Moroccan potato in the pocket of my jeans. Sadly, the officer found the hashish almost immediately and began swearing at me in Spanish, telling me I'd made a big mistake and would pay for it dearly.

It was a stroke of luck that we had Jen on board, because she spoke their language fluently. Displaying all the charm of a belly-dancing goddess on a continental Saturday night, Jenny reasoned with the guards, telling them that our group ran one of the island's best-known club nights, and that we brought valuable income and tourist activity into the community. I suppose we were looking at payola, but there you go!

The officer looked over at me, eyeing my black suit. Taking a second glance, he took a miniature bullet packed with Charlie from Thomo's pocket and placed it on the car. A shudder went up and down Thomo's body. Another officer picked up the small brown plastic bottle, examining the medicine-like container before putting it back and rubbing him down. All eyes were on me: the officers were angry I'd brought the puff into their country and things were looking bad. On the other hand, Jen knew the laws of the land, and kept on saying they couldn't arrest me for such a tiny amount. By this point I didn't know what to believe. I was still in shock at them not realising the tiny brown bottle packed with white powder was an illegal narcotic. Whatever, amazingly we were let off with a serious warning. For some reason I was told to take a taxi to the club and not drive. I stuck everything back into my pockets, including the high-grade hashish, and Thomo quietly drove off. I was very relieved I didn't get a full search, because I was holding much more.

Immediately a minibus driven by Matt was flagged down. He'd often take people to the clubs and was much cheaper than a taxi. His van was a blue VW thing with a pink 'Manumission' logo on each side. The Guardia pulled him over at least once a day and searched everyone present for drugs. Under normal circumstances I'd never get into the van, but I needed to reach the old town in time for the meeting. There were two other passengers, who welcomed me on board. Within minutes of driving through San Ann's busy roads, however, a Guardia Civil jeep started tailing us. Paranoid they'd find the secret stash, I slipped on to the floor and pulled out the big wrap. An eighth of gear is a lot to sniff at once, but like a totally mad fucker I began shovelling mountains up my nostrils and whacking it out to everybody in the vehicle. Soon enough, the evidence was far gone – the trouble was, so were we! Dibble continued to follow, before taking a slip-road in another direction. What a bummer!

I was gutted: all my stash, all my sanity, gone in one dodgy turning. My usual, outgoing character sank into a miserable, pathetic, Charlied-up introverted maniac who was completely on edge. The night ahead promised to be a personal disaster. There was nothing for it: I'd have to go home, go to bed, drop a few Temazepams and crash for England. The others hadn't even reached the club before I was back home under lock and key.

Top night out? Even thinking about it now, I'm grinding my teeth!

# **9** Rip Curl

One night in '95, we all went to Mambo's for a drink and to watch Ibiza's famous sunset. We'd been on a two-day bender, cruising from party to party before ending up at the Kiss FM villa with Bobby, Steve and Rico. Javier, the owner, was a cool dude who loved seeing happy faces in his bar. There were more promoters and DJs per square inch here than anywhere on the island. The list of them read like chapters from the dance-scene Bible: Havin' It, Eden, Cream, Rude, Up Yer Ronson, Back to Basics, Clockwork Orange, Love to Be, The Leisure Lounge, The Ministry of Sound. Mambo was a regular meeting place, where everyone gathered to find out who was on the island, what was going on there or just to have the proverbial 'quiet drink' – which usually meant the inmates getting trashed.

However, despite a tantalising range of dishes, the only fare we were generally found sampling in San Antonio was at Mambo, Café del Mar and the Kanya Bar. We tended to spend most of our time in Ibiza Town.

The sleepless days were catching up with me a bit that night as I watched the marvel of the sun setting, and the little man in the boat, who'd wait until the golden ball of fire was balanced on the horizon before sailing back and forth in front of the beautiful vision. He would have provided a perfect photo opportunity for anyone from Johnny Quicksnaps to David flippin' Bailey. Lovely sight.

My body had been sending alarm signals to my brain for over six hours, but I continued regardless. I was lost in deep thought as I watched the sun silently disappear. It was a wonderful, but temporary peace. The drugs I had devoured in the past were beginning to affect me mentally. It wasn't anything too noticeable, and usually amounted to a few mild hallucinations followed by dramatic flashbacks, but it was starting to get worrying. My near-death experience at the might of the Indian Ocean had left a stark, chilling impression locked within the vaults of my Ecstasy-scrambled memory.

I've always loved the sea and water sports, and no, I'm not taking the piss, you perverts! I'd only recently qualified as a scuba diver. It's all in the genes, I reckon. My mum – a Piscean – has always been addicted to the sea. When we were kids on the beach, she would throw the whole family into the water at the earliest opportunity. Long-distance swimming was my mum's thing, and I remembered this as I gazed right out to sea, staring so far that all I could see were tiny figures surrounded by dark-green water.

The sea would never scare us as children, because Mum would embark on a cross-Atlantic swim each time it came into view. If anything, it made us more determined to perfect a strong stroke, so that we too could be out there swimming alongside boats with our old dear.

I'd done a number of spectacular dives around the globe and you might say I fair fancied myself as a pukka diver. But I had been in dangerously close contact with death on a number of occasions. An early warning sign of a flashback usually came as a shudder through my entire body, like an unholy stampede running over my grave. Then, in a split second, I was back at Bondi Beach, Australia – famous around the world for great surf, hot chicks and international beach bums, and unforgettable for me for one of my most horrifying encounters with death.

Bondi Beach was – and is – a huge stretch of sand, which on a hot day caters for thousands and thousands of people. Every year this section of the ocean claims at least 50 lives, due to rough waters and individuals inexperienced in the unpredictable movement of the surf. One momentary lapse of personal safety and you could easily be history. From an aerial view, the beach resembles a half-moon shape, near the centre of which are two red flags about a hundred yards apart. All swimmers are urged to stay between the flags whilst in the water. The vigilant lifeguards are particularly strict about these rules, and keep a constant watch for anyone crossing the human-imposed barriers.

One day I was with a group of friends, knocking about at the far end of the beach near some rocks. We were just kicking back in the sun, smoking, talking and taking in the sights of silicon valley. Whilst we chatted, hundreds of surfers would manipulate the great white waters to conquer and skilfully ride each wave with the zest and skill of salmon. The sparkling cool water was hard to resist on such a beautiful day. After a while, I decided to sample the pleasures myself and waded into the ocean – just past my knobbly knees. As each wave came into shore, I'd dive into the swell, appearing on the other side with my feet sinking in the sand.

Enjoying *Baywatch* dive techniques took my mind off the dangers of not swimming between the flags. My mind started to dare me: It can't be as bad as they say. My subconscious demons were invading my consciousness and goading me, on what could easily have been one last, fateful journey.

As time flew by, the swells grew bigger and stronger. A monster wave approached the beach as I shaped up and dived into the surf at an angle. It felt like my whole body was being held beneath the water: skimming the seabed, I was suddenly propelled upward to the surface. There was no longer any sand under my feet, and as I turned to face the shore I could feel a strange fear gripping my soul. The unknown, mysterious great ocean had carried me almost 40 yards out. I knew this was serious and so I tried swimming to the beach, but the force of the current meant that, instead of moving forward, I was just swimming on the spot. In fact, I suddenly realised I was floating further out to sea. This wasn't just serious; this was fucking terrifying.

Waves measuring six feet or more in height kept crashing down on my head, each time forcing me underwater. I'd tried riding the crest of a wave, giving it all I had, but still I remained stationary, trapped between a mountain range of salt water, with nothing to be seen in front of or behind me. My exhausted body ached with pain, my fading heartbeat composed a drum roll that junglists and samplers would die for, and my puff-wearied lungs were on the brink of collapsing. I screamed for help.

'HELLP. HELLPP! I'M DRAAAAAWNNNNNNNNING...'

But nobody heard me.

My cries could not be audible over the waves crashing against rocks that were only yards away. The water appeared to be moving both forward and backward simultaneously, while at the same time sucking me beneath its raging torrent. This was an unholy battle against one of the earth's most powerful elements. It lasted on and on, probably for around 20 minutes – but it felt like an eternity. After a while, my body began to show the dreaded signs of seizure. Every joint was slowly failing. A wave smashed into my stationary, slumped body, sending it shuddering into the depths. I did – and could do – nothing to stop a looming, seemingly inevitable death, and could only look up helplessly at the surface while moving deeper and deeper to meet my maker. I was painfully aware of my forthcoming fate but, perhaps strangely, didn't think it would be a painful death. Tired and physically drained as I was, I thought death would come peacefully. Perhaps if I'd been screaming or kicking for dear life it might have been very different, but by the time I finally went under, my weary body was so shattered that life would pass away in the blink of an eye. It was almost as if I was in a blissful, trancelike state. I started hallucinating, awash with strange thoughts, like the one that foresaw a giant dolphin swimming up from the depths and taking me to Atlantis.

Experiencing my last moments on earth, though, I couldn't quite believe I was about to die on Bondi Beach, and started thinking about my mother. I can never quite explain what happened next, but it seemed as if a last superhuman, and indeed subconscious, super-strength had surged through my body. Somehow I managed to swim back up to the surface and began frantically flapping for the shore, although I still wasn't getting any nearer. My last attempt at saving my fading life had sadly amounted to nothing, and a massive wave sent me crashing under once more. The grim reaper had a hold of me and I was suddenly utterly terrified. My life and family flashed in front of my open, bloodshot eyes.

'I cannot die! I cannot die! I have to go home!'

My inner voices were pleading.

In tune with the elements, I swam up to the surface and started screaming. A surfer skimmed the water towards me, shouting and swearing as he came. He asked me to swim with him to the beach, but I told him my body was incapable of moving a muscle.

'Why ain't ya swimming between the flags, ya stupid Pom?' he cried, exasperated. 'You come over here and think you can do what you please. I'm missing fucking good surf out there, mate!'

I didn't know which was the more pathetic: the surfer's concern for his riding time or my own sorry state.

Pleading with my reluctant rescuer, I managed to convince the blond, surfer bimbo to take me on board and back into safer waters. Three lifeguards stood at the water's edge, along with all my startled friends, who'd only just noticed the commotion. Once on dry sand, I fell into a heap and a deep sleep for an hour. When I woke, I realised these three things: that the sea is more dangerous than drugs; that I was lucky to be alive; and, most worryingly of all, that God exists.

Worrying? Oh yeah, because the Church of England lied. He isn't a spiritual deity or an old man with a beard at all.

He's a fuckin' Aussie surfer!

# **10** Acid Daze

Drugs are integral to our society. One of the undeniable and saddening home truths facing anti-pharmaceutical campaigners of all types is that people just love popping pills. They're a part of our lives from early childhood – whether they're vitamins, aspirins or even pills we give to the dog. They're all tiny, usually white, deceptively innocent-looking capsules, so that it's hardly surprising people grow up thinking there can't be that much difference between something that lowers your blood pressure and something that gets you off your nut. Often they're the same flippin' pills anyway. One person's 'caring' sedative Temazepam is another's 'evil' smack-substitute. Some kids raid their mother's bathroom cabinets for Valium, barbs or Tuinol. Later on they might prefer Ecstasy, puff or rocky, whilst many toot coke, smoke crack or stick needles into their veins. There are a hundred times as many people physically and mentally addicted to alcohol, anti-depressants and nicotine as there are to heroin or Charlie. Different strokes for different folks, right? Sadly, many of us grow up to learn the differences the hard way.

Casper's crew loved tripping – and I don't mean nature rambles. Their life's work was to track down and consume hallucinogenics, whether they were synthetically manufactured or grew naturally in abstract parts of the world. Tripping can be a fascinating process, like a massive scientific experiment in which you're the willing guinea pig. The key to enjoying it is somehow to harness the mind-boggling interaction between the regular areas of the brain and the bombardment of new (il)logical thought patterns. It's amazing to try and adapt the power of the mind to questions that have arisen from the depths of the subconscious. Surely this is what taking drugs is all about. Why else would anyone take drugs, if it wasn't to enlighten or enrich their lives?

Casper's group had long since adopted this theory of LSD and came over like a bunch of raving Timothy Learys. When I hooked up with them in '95, they'd been all over and had the stories to prove it. They'd been at wild full-moon parties in India, had gone a bit in Goa and had more than a good time in Thailand. Been there, seen that, climbed in, sailed out and came back with stories to tell. They'd caned it so much that music itself was a heavy trip for them – they preferred the cooler, softer, less imposing beauty of pure ambience. It helped them to concentrate.

On these acid-fuelled quests of self-exploration, the group would share dreams with one another, sometimes astrally projected, in another time and another world. They weren't bothered about not having the riches of wealth, because they had the riches of knowledge. These guys were fuckin' deep, but spiritual – the kind of people who could slow down your whole metabolism just by talking to you. Whenever they were around me it was impossible not to be affected by the strange atmosphere of calmness and cool.

The crew had arrived in Ibiza in '95 following a spiritual mission through Mexico, then across to India and up to Thailand and Vietnam. Since touching down they'd been taking nothing but Blue Meanies, the notorious South American mushrooms believed to contain mysterious powers, and used by the Incas for thousands of years. Legend has it that if you use a certain amount you'll actually meet the spirit guides who accompany your soul through the Afterlife. Beats taking the train from Victoria to Brighton, anyways.

As the crew told it, the trick was to ask the right questions so as to receive the right answers. Then you had to remember everything you'd seen – no matter how bananas – and take these visions to an Indian shaman for interpretation. Sadly, no matter how hard they tried, none of the crew got to meet any kind of spiritual guide – he probably took one good look at them and yelled, 'Bloody drug-addled tourists!'

A good friend of mine called Carlos had given the crew the

full use of his huge villa while he was off on business in Miami. Before that, they'd been living in beach huts, shabby hotel rooms and their own tents for months. The funny thing was: none of them actually wanted to sleep in the house, so instead they set up camp outside in the valley, with a fantastic sea view. One night they were buzzing a bit too much and decided to go into the house in search of some munchies. There was a massive fridge in the kitchen. The wine cellar was targeted and a rack of red brought upstairs to the main living quarters. It wasn't as if they were taking the piss: Carlos had got the provisions in for them anyway. In another room there was a giant, round TV hooked up to a Bang & Olufsen sound system. The electronic gadgetry was perfectly suited to the acoustically designed room and enhanced the group's buzz by 50 per cent. Carlos loved dance music and most of his CD collection was made up of various dance compilations from all round the world. He certainly knew his stuff and could tell you the artist, producer, label and time of release of almost any tune he heard. He should have been in the music business, really, but instead chose to sell shares on the stock exchange and build his own empire. He was an ambitious man.

When Carlos was at home, one of his ridiculously expensive tables played host to a small box, which was supposed to have belonged to one of the pharaohs. Now it held . . . . the drugs! Whenever Carlos had company, the box was left open on the table – like a narcotic selection box: top-quality Peruvian flake, California Ecstasy and Caribbean smoke. Most temptingly of all, a secret compartment held some original super-strong Pink Floyd acid tabs, a hundred in all, which had cost Carlos no less than $3,000. They'd been kept in a special plastic casing in someone's fridge for nearly 30 years, which had apparently kept the trips in all their former glory, but it didn't seem to have done much for Carlos's bank account.

As one of the man's close friends, I knew the secret combination to the safe where the box was neatly stashed, so it seemed only reasonable to open the miniature mummy's casket and let the group enjoy its contents. The South American flake elevated the mushrooms to new heights, so the crew dropped more and more. It wasn't long before everyone had totally lost it, and started re-enacting scenes from films they'd seen at the cinema. *Romeo and Juliet* was squeezed down to about three minutes, before Juliet gave in and jumped naked into the swimming pool with Al Pacino, who wasn't even in the film! I knew it was time for trouble when Demi Moore started being stripped by The Terminator. Thank God, or Aussie surfers, nobody thought of re-enacting that scene from *The Alien*.

Each film star was mimicked to perfection and everyone stayed in character for hours. John Wayne – me, unsurprisingly – pushed past Calamity Jane and sat down, staring at the stereo. Tarzan, Pamela Anderson, Mr Bean and Batman announced they were about to perform a show. Grandmaster Flash and Melle Mel's 'White Lines' rang out, which seemed to fit the occasion perfectly. As the music played, waves of sound seemed to move through the air, causing visible ripples that gently shook my body. I could see waves created by people's movements hovering like heatwaves above the ground, before disappearing through the walls. Well weird.

I jumped to my feet and ran outside to follow the sounds as they passed through the concrete walls. From the front window I could see actual words and musical notes coming from the speakers in streams of music. Everybody was speaking with animated words, which floated to the ceiling and stayed there. I started laughing heartily, and everyone turned to face me.

'Are you OK?'

The words came flying towards me and seemed to settle on the ceiling. I wasn't sure if I should be exultant or terrified. Each time someone talked, I 'saw' the words, yet they'd vanish with a clap of my hand and the 'sound' would return to normal.

'Wow,' I said. 'That was fucking amazing!'

Around this time Calamity Jane had a great idea.

'Let's go to Manumission at Ku! It's a huge party night for thousands of people. Let's do it!'

We were exalted by this: in fact, it seemed like the best idea we'd ever heard. So that settled it, we were going to Ku.

Although Carlos only stayed at the house for three months a year, he had two cars in the garage. One was a Range Rover and the other a BMW convertible. Still singing loudly, we made our way to the club. Ku was a hedonist's paradise. Although it looked something like a bank from outside, past the large glass entrance lay another world. It was possibly one of the biggest clubs in the world, and regularly played host to thousands of party animals. You didn't need drugs – the vibe was enough. But I suppose if you had them, it wouldn't do any harm.

We arrived to find a full-on water fight erupting between hordes of people diving about in a swimming pool, whilst another 50 or so danced on a platform above the pool. In sync with the music, a fountain of water burst into the air, thoroughly drenching people in its brilliant blue spray. We all dropped a Cali and hit the dance floor, whilst Al Pacino and Batman went off to find the toilets.

There were two people in the queue in front of them, but Batman was bursting. Ten minutes elapsed, after which one of the guys in the queue started banging on the cubicle door.

The toilets were situated in a really awkward place. Whoever designed them must have been totally off their nut.

'How can the dumb fucks put a john next to the dance floor?' moaned Al Pacino, as all around them started laughing.

'What's going on?' asked Batman.

It was only as they walked away that they realised the source of the amusement. The 'cubicle' wasn't a toilet at all, but some kind of stage prop in the shape of a Gents bog. They looked at each other and collapsed with laughter at their utterly addled state.

Back upstairs, Pamela Anderson was so deep in conversation with Mr Bean that she didn't notice the transvestite swinging on a trapeze above them or the guy dressed as a wizard who appeared to be floating over the balcony. Bean had the right hump with the fella in the wizard costume. He thought he was wearing a Ku-Klux-Klan grand-wizard uniform and kept shouting obscenities each time he passed.

'You're fucking Ku-Klux-Klan, you fucking shit cunt.'

The aggression soon passed in the heat of the cacophony.

I wandered through the haze with Pam. Eventually we came across a guy sitting in an armchair watching the blank screen of a television in front of him. What a weird dude! He was watching intently, as if he could see something we couldn't, and maybe he could. Soon everyone else sat around the dude and also gazed at the blank screen. Every few seconds people would clap, as if they were watching a brilliant sports move or something; but no matter what state they were in, surely most people realised the TV was blank. After a short while, around a hundred people were gathered round the screen, cheering and jeering each other's imaginary teams, and hardly noticing as a transvestite Mrs Merton-lookalike cleaner in an apron and rubber gloves started cleaning a small coffee table by the set.

The other clubbers thought the scene was crazy, but no one cared; the only issue important to them was their imaginary team winning the Cup. The shocked hippies around couldn't contain their laughter. I must admit, I've been involved in some mad things in my time, but this was pushing even my limits.

Distracted – and still half-locked in my imaginary role as John Wayne – I started getting down with a tiny woman who was seriously giving it some in the dance stakes. She grabbed me round the neck, wrapping her long, lithe legs around my waist. My mates were all laughing, but I couldn't say no to the surreal phantasm of it all. Here I was: off my banana in a nightclub, with a swimming pool, giant fountains, 8,000 people and a sexy midget who was trying to do something with my waist. I always did love surreal shit like this.

Eventually, she kissed me on the cheek and her dance troupe moved on. Convinced they'd won by at least ten goals, the happy hippies continued touring the club. Carlos had honorary membership cards to every club on the island and they generally allowed you a free drink at every bar in the gaff. After counting twelve, we ended up in a room at the back of the club. Massive windows stretched along one side and presented a fantastic view of the colourful skies illuminated by the sunrise. Awesome!

The music here was much better than that in the main room, as the DJ played a wicked set of all old stuff from the Acid House days. The atmosphere was near enough the same as it was back then, with everyone on the same cheerful buzz and soaked with sweat from dancing themselves stupid. We were the last to leave, ambling through the now empty club, which had suddenly transformed from a heaven to a morgue.

Our motors stuck out like sore thumbs in the car park. Where the fuck had everybody gone?

We clambered into the vehicles as I led the way out on to the main road. By the main entrance there was an old man with a shoebox in his lap.

'Wanna lift?' I enquired.

We quickly nicknamed him 'Grasshopper', as he jumped into the Range Rover. He didn't say anything, just pointed in the direction of the old town, which we had to pass anyway. He wore a vegetable sack sewn together Babylonian-style and looked weird and otherworldy, just staring silently out of the window. Assuming he didn't speak English, the Brat Pack – still firmly locked in character – greeted him in eight different accents. That didn't work. Next we tried a 'Hello' in eight different languages. No response. Around this time we started thinking: what was in that box?

Eventually I could contain myself no longer.

'Señor, what you have in the box – your wife?'

Laughter erupted as I added a less impertinent, 'No, seriously, what's in the box?'

It seemed a weird, closely guarded secret.

'*Spaniloa, no comprenda*!' he insisted, although I was pretty sure he knew full well what I was asking.

The girls in the Range Rover kept poking me in the back as an encouragement.

'*Qué pasa, señor?*'

Grasshopper put the box on the floor, and his feet on top of it. There was no way he was letting us look at it.

Suddenly there was a shout.

'Heads up, everyone, police roadblock – there's been an accident. Hide the gear!'

The early-morning traffic almost came to a standstill as we inched along at under 5 m.p.h. Suddenly Grasshopper turned to the others, bowed his head politely and jumped out of the vehicle.

Calamity Jane watched as the frail-looking but fit man walked across a field.

'Hold yer horses, partners, where's the box? He's not holding the box!'

I picked it up from the floor. Something about it disturbed me.

'We'll have a look inside when we get home,' I said.

I took the scenic route, which added half an hour to the journey but relaxed everyone. Al Pacino noticed that I seemed to be driving in time to the music, which caused a few problems when it came to a full-on techno mix!

Al nearly had a nervous breakdown as William Horace tried to overtake us on a very narrow road.

'STOP, STOOP, STOOP!'

I slammed on the brakes, sending the rear occupants into the front seats. Al Pacino calmly said that it might be a better idea to play the Café del Mar album. So we continued home to the soothing but still often breakneck sounds of Balearic beats, and I'm afraid to say I was still driving like a maniac.

'Who wants tea?' asked Barbarella, back in the kitchen. Everyone was pretty shattered, especially poor old Mr Bean, who'd had to grunt and gurn like Rowan Atkinson's bananas character – on drugs! – for all of twelve hours. Tarzan couldn't work out how we'd kept it up for so long. The other clubbers hadn't recognised his character at all and thought he couldn't speak!

Tarzan pulled out a money bag filled with Meanies and poured them into the kettle. He rubbed his hands like a mad scientist as Barbarella made the tea. Then we got stuck into the puff, quickly getting stoned. Barbarella never smoked, insisting that grass, hash and hydro had no effect on her. This bothered me, because I knew it couldn't be true, especially the stuff we were smoking. I'd been puffing for years and you couldn't tell me it didn't affect you – and this weed was so strong it could knock out a bull. It was time to call her bluff.

'You know what I think, Barbarella?'

'Oh, here we go . . . What do you think, John Wayne?'

'I bet you're one of those girls who totally loses it when they've had a puff,' I said. 'I know you can handle class-A, but class-B . . . I bet you can't handle this joint.'

I held up a pre-rolled big boy, with the minimum tobacco and maximum Jamaican Sensee.

'I've done it so many times before and proved everyone wrong that I'm not going to fall for that one,' she insisted.

'You mean you're afraid?' I scoffed.

I knew it would get to her. Barbarella was the independent type, who liked to boast she could do anything a man could. Off-the-cuff remarks from her male friends only made her more determined.

'I've got an idea,' she countered. 'If I smoke the whole joint, you have to drop another two Calis.'

Crikey!

'I don't mind doing that,' I spluttered, 'but only if it doesn't affect you. Otherwise all bets are off.'

I handed her the spliff and lighter, which she immediately put into action. Everybody was impressed – she was halfway through the spliff and she hadn't even coughed. As she finished it, Barbarella calmly put it in the ashtray and brought a glass of peach schnapps and two California Ecstasy tabs over to me.

'Well now, John Wayne. Looks like we got ourselves a situation here,' she stated. 'We know a fine, outstanding member of the community like yourself ain't gonna back out on yer word . . . are ya?'

As much as I wanted to, I knew I couldn't back out of this one. Half an hour later I was lying on the sofa wishing I'd kept my big mouth shut, whilst Barbarella was taken ill.

At least I found this very funny.

'I knew it would catch up with you,' I laughed.

'My tits are hurting. I can't breathe,' sobbed Barbarella. 'No, really, I need a hospital, I think it's serious.'

The Terminator, William Horace and Mr Bean joined me and pissed themselves, giving the girls – who were concerned – the right hump. Looking back, it wasn't that we were behaving like schoolboys (much), it was more that the mushrooms (and, in my case, the Es) were playing havoc with our brain tissue. Batman turned the stereo up – it was a Phil Collins number – as we took deep breaths and sang out loud.

'If you told me you were drowning, I would not lend a hand. I've seen your face before, my love, I don't know if you know who I am. Well I was there and I saw what you did, saw it with my own two eyes . . .'

Suddenly a strong gust of air blew through the room, stopping the singing in its tracks. It seemed to come from inside the house somewhere.

'Hey, guys, look what I've got!'

Pam came running into the room with the mysterious shoebox, which we'd all managed to forget about in the commotion.

'Open it, open it!' insisted William.

I remembered my earlier concern and replied, 'I don't think we should interfere with it. Let's try and find Grasshopper and give it back to him.'

There was – I knew – something odd about this box.

'Are you mad? We'll never find him now,' said Pam. 'Anyway, I think we deserve to know.'

I was strangely traumatised.

'Look, I'm being really serious about this. We shouldn't touch it; there's something not right about it.'

I stepped away from Pam, as Al Pacino shared in my concern about the contents of the box.

Suddenly, Barbarella – now feeling very light-headed – grabbed the box and ripped the top off.

'It's empty!' she shrieked. 'That's funny, it felt like something was inside, but now it feels a lot lighter.'

Immediately the temperature in the room dropped. Stranger still, the mood of those in the room changed. We sat there staring at the walls in silence, until we were jolted by the sound of footsteps upstairs. A few of us, feeling more normal, decided to investigate, leaving the girls huddled together on the sofa. We searched all the rooms but found nothing.

Then the screaming started.

'HELLLLLLLLPPPPPPPP! HELLLLLLLLLLPPPPP! HELLLLLLLLLLLLLLLLPPPPP!'

The girls were screaming so loudly that the waves echoed around the building, making a deafening sound. We rushed downstairs to find them cowering in a corner of the living room, visibly shaken.

'What's happened? What the hell's going on?'

Nikki (aka Calamity Jane) told us that a ghost had brushed past her and Kerry (aka Juliet) and had disappeared into an adjoining room. As Kerry told it, they couldn't see what had touched them, but felt its unmistakable presence as the entity roamed the room.

Steve (aka Peter Pan), Cazwell (aka William Horace), Femi (Terminator), Ricardo (Al Pacino), Paul (Romeo), Andy

(Batman), Glenn (Mr Bean) and I barged into the other room as the girls ran screaming into the kitchen. Of course, there was nothing to be seen in there, even if an unidentified spook was doing handstands and blowing kisses in our faces. How on earth could we tell?

We went into the kitchen and found the girls armed to the teeth.

'We want to go back to our tents,' yelped Emma, who was certainly no longer Pamela Anderson.

'OK,' I said. 'Grab the gear, we're outta here.'

Like sailors jumping ship, we went back to the camp a mere five minutes from the house. Everyone was particularly tense, especially the girls, who refused to discuss what had just happened. A couple of hours later everything had returned more or less to normal, although the girls were all squeezed together in one tent, coming down from the drugs. The rest of us lay in the sunshine, drenched in sunblock and heading into semi-comas.

I was the first to wake. It was now pitch-black outside, and I must have slept for hours. As I rubbed the cold from my eyes, I started to piece together bits from earlier in the day, glancing at the house in the foreground.

'What the fuck?'

I almost shat myself on the spot.

A blue light was illuminating the front of the whole building room by room; it was as if something was in there floating around, although for me it could only mean one thing. Someone was in the house. I tried to wake the others, but it was no use, they were cabbaged.

I rolled a spliff as I debated with myself whether to approach the house. I felt responsible. It was Carlos's home and if something was wrong, it was my duty to investigate. Prising a Hallowe'en knife from Nikki's hand, I headed towards the unknown. A knife was the least useful weapon to warn off ghosts, but it made me feel stronger and more confident. After all, it wasn't necessarily a spirit and could easily have been burglars, or something else. Whatever the case, I felt ready for anything . . . or so I thought.

The blue light appeared to move faster and faster as I warily approached the house. It was as if I was being watched from every window, and whoever was watching me was whizzing from room to room. I took a deep breath and crept in through the back door. The house was freezing, yet it wasn't that cold outside. None of the lights worked, so I had to search each room with a small torch and weapon raised. There was nothing on the ground floor, so I made my way upstairs. I could hear whispering, which got louder and louder as an icy chill ran over my skin. I lost my bottle. As I leapt over the banister, running towards the (open) front door, I ran smack-bang into a tiny figure. In a state of utter panic I brought my knife-hand down hard.

With reflexes like a snake, the tiny man stopped my arm with his foot and quickly took the weapon from my hand.

'Please, sir, I've come for my box.'

It was the old man.

'What the fuck are you doing here? Has Carlos paid you to wind us up? You could have been killed!'

He asked me to follow him and said that there wasn't much time.

'Bollocks,' I said, still trembling. 'I'm not going anywhere with you. Go and get your box yourself.'

Grasshopper went into the house and emerged minutes later with the supposedly empty shoebox. He thanked me and walked off into the darkness of the night. As I cautiously ventured into the reception area, there was an immediate change in temperature and the mood of the building felt much lighter. Even the electricity worked. Whatever 'it' was, I knew 'it' had gone. Back at the camp, no one apart from Nikki and Kerry would believe my story, but I swore to them that it was true.

Whether they believed me or not, every single one of them had left for Thailand within days.

# **11** A Letter From London

Sometimes in Ibiza it's easy to lose yourself in the island's barmy lifestyle. You can go for weeks without a care in the world. Sometimes, though, it's good to have a jolt from the real world.

This is a letter that arrived in Ibiza, postmarked from the UK capital.

Hey Bro,

How are you? I hope things are going well, little brother. You're really lucky to be over there in the sun; it's only been eight weeks since the family last saw your ugly face! They all miss you and send their love . . . you know what they're like.

Nothing much to report as far as England is concerned. I'm still working hard trying to make a decent living for myself. It's fucking hard, bro', but I'm getting on with it. The streets are getting worse by the day. I had to escort our baby sister to school this morning. Some fucking bloke keeps staring at her on the bus; he doesn't say anything, he just stares. Fucking weirdo. He's been doing it for a few weeks now, but yesterday he decided to get off the bus at the same stop as Maria and followed her to school. He's really frightened her, the poor thing. I woke up this morning with the sole intention of smashing the cunt's head in. It's so easy for our lives to change drastically – I'm prepared to go to prison for the paedophile prick, but he didn't show.

I'll be with her every day this week until I see him. You know I'm a hard worker: never been in trouble with the law in my life. But that's how easy it is – a singular act by someone I don't even know is about to change my quiet life. I'm going to hurt this guy, even if it's right there on the bus. Anyway, don't you worry about it, I'm dealing with the problem. I hope you're not doing too many drugs, little brother. I can't stop you from doing them, but I do worry about you, kid. The things people do for the sake of a buzz is unbelievable. What a high price to pay, but I bet death is the ultimate high for you lot.

I was with Michael in Holland last weekend: everyone out there is talking about some sort of Ecstasy shortage. There's some major scams going on over there, bro', pills being made with no MDDA, or whatever it's called. But the one I have to warn you about is PMA. Please, little brother, for your own sake and your family's, don't take this tablet. I'm begging you. I've never had a pop at you for taking drugs before, but this is different. The stuff is poisonous and kills. I know Es are lethal and kill people, but not like this drug does. It's nicknamed 'Death', for God's sake. Nine people who live in the same neighbourhood in Australia have already died and the drug is on its way to the major European cities. It's five times more powerful than Ecstasy and looks just like E. You've got to be careful what you're taking, Bro, I'm begging you. Your mum is so worried about you, she can't get to sleep until the early hours of the morning. If anything happened to you it would destroy our family.

Do you understand what I'm saying? You don't just risk your life, you're risking all our lives. Because your mum and sisters would lose their mind, and I fucking mean that. Don't you be so fucking selfish. We all lead our own lives, but if you were taking drugs and something went wrong, you may as well say we all die with you. Except for us it would be a living nightmare, as we'd be constantly reminded of you by everything around us. That's what we have to deal with: I want to lead my own life too, Bro. I don't want to spend the rest of my days looking after a mentally disturbed family, because of you. Give yourself – and give us – a chance to lead a happy life, without worrying about you dying from a chain reaction caused by taking a fake pill, or any pill. I know you're on holiday, bro', and you don't want to hear this, but just think about it.

I have to go now, so be careful; always wear a rubber, and make sure you eat.

From your big brother in wet & cold London.

PS Do the right thing, bro.

I didn't.

# **12** Cream Closing

Club opening and closing parties are easily the best of the season. Attending them is an annual ritual for thousands of clubbers, who look to the start of each season as a fresh beginning, to be climaxed by a hedonistic celebration at the end of each exemplary Iberian summer. Individuals who participate in these annual festivities of love are usually hyped-up to the max and ready for anything.

'Cream' was hosted at Ku (Privilege) by Amanda and Jason, although he left mid-season. They had a good year at Ku on Thursday nights, with the club packed solid each week and impressive DJ line-ups thrashing out banging sets of house music. One night, Kylie Minogue was brought over to perform live to an 8,000-strong crowd of international clubbers. Surprisingly enough she kicked arse, and had at least a couple of thousand singing along with her, which was quite some achievement. This wasn't some pop venue full of squares who'd only just discovered dance music – the majority of Ibiza's clubbers really know their shit and wouldn't accept a half-hearted performance from anybody, no matter who they were. Which is why nearly every DJ, band or vocalist wants to perform live in the Balearics – succeed there and you can do it anywhere.

It was gonna be a big night at Cream, and everyone hurried round the villa trying to get dressed. We'd been sleeping all day and all night after getting in late from the Rock Bar. Nick and Sid, the owners, were proper nutters who were game for anything and got our crew right at it. We downed bottle after bottle of schnapps, chased by numerous brain-searing rounds of chapitos. Ohh, my head!

A huge American battleship had moored in the dock for the night, meaning that groups of marines were everywhere we looked. Driving and walking round in packs of twelve, the soldiers were either trying to impress or intimidate holidaymakers. Just watching the way they bowled about gave casual drinkers good reason to take the piss out of them. What with their brilliant white *Officer and a Gentleman* uniforms, the marines gave off some really bad karma.

Over the road from the bar, an orderly queue waited patiently for a public telephone. I sat upstairs in the bar, observing the marines from an open window.

Suddenly I yelled 'YMCA!' at the top of my voice. The marines all stared at the bar, but couldn't identify the culprit, as the 50 or so people outside struggled to contain their bouts of delirious laughter. Each time calm was restored, I'd do it again.

'YMCA!'

This went on for about ten minutes, by which time the marines were getting seriously pissed off. A group of them came into the bar and upstairs, where another bar, pool table and the toilets were situated. The other drinkers – about 20 in all – were in on the joke, so when the stiffs came into the bar in single file, the whole room went quiet. The troops stood, agitated, staring at the onlookers before turning and leaving. As the last one disappeared from the door, I did it again.

'YMCA.'

Quick as a flash they piled back into the bar, shouting obscenities at the 'wossie who wouldn't put his balls where his mouth was'.

I may sometimes be a bit stupid, but I'm never that stupid! There were at least 2,000 men on that battleship and there was no way I was taking them on. I decided to give the YMCA shouts a rest and disappeared.

Having woken up at 11.30 p.m., the rush was on to get something to eat before the restaurants in Ibiza Town closed. I shot off in a motor with my pals Dominic, Ed, Tank and Windross and caught Westside just as it was about to close. The owners were an English couple, really nice people who'd go out of their way to look after regular customers. The wife took the orders and played the perfect hostess while the husband served up the extremely mouth-watering cuisine. The chef had a habit of coming out and asking whether the food was to our liking.

Still woozy from the night before, a hair of the dog seemed most appropriate before we started on the booze once more. About fifteen minutes later the girls turned up, moaning and groaning that no hot water was left for them to shower with. After finishing a fine meal and the good dog's hairy bits, we all breezed through the Rock Bar and drove down to Privilege.

The night was in full swing. Some of our mates cavorted on the balcony opposite the DJ console; the champagne and drugs were flowing freely. Anton le Pirate (see *Class of '88*), Neil Armstrong and Paul were blind-drunk and in their stupor contemplated diving from the balcony into the swimming pool. It wasn't quite daredevil status, but dangerous enough: the pool was merely five feet deep, and in a decade of visiting Ibiza, nobody had ever seen anyone dive from the balcony.

It wasn't a straightforward dive. First they'd have to find enough launch power to carry them five yards out from the balcony, then down into the water, without smashing their heads on the bottom. Everyone stood around open-mouthed, pleading with them not to do it, but within half an hour the daredevilish trio had stripped to their boxers and, in military single file, took flight – amazingly, landing safely in the pool. Each time one of them landed, they'd be dragged out by furious security guards, to ripples of applause.

'Are you totally crazy?' yelled the guards.

You and I know the answer to that one. Whatever, they were kicked out of the club.

I was on a strong buzz that night, but I got bored and went for a walk around the club. Soon enough I bumped into some mates, who were toasting someone's birthday. They necked a bottle of champagne and started dancing about. As I was savouring the champers, two particularly provocatively dressed girls marched straight up to me, saying 'Hi'. My pals looked on open-mouthed as both desirable females rubbed their prized assets against my quavering body. They said they'd come from Germany and were employed as dancers at Pacha. I bought another bottle and they led me upstairs.

Shortly afterwards I found myself on a small outdoor terrace, like a garden. There was no one else in sight and it was pitch-dark. After taking me to a hidden spot where nobody could see us, the girls took a few shots of bubbly before one of them began caressing my groin. I have to confess, for a second I thought that either the drugs were doing my head in or this was a serious wind-up! It wasn't (I suppose I must be fairly handsome ... in a certain sort of light). Anyway, quickly enough the other girl stripped totally naked and joined us. I was still consciously – and probably subconsciously – shocked, and couldn't climax for ages. Undisturbed for over an hour, we all started laughing and fell about the place as we got dressed.

As we returned to the birthday bunch, my friends could only express jealous amazement at the obvious signs that the three of us were now particularly intimate. The girls' dancing was more erotic than ever, but they had eyes only for me. They obviously thought: Hey, that's the guy that will one day write *Class of '88*! Ha – or maybe not.

We exchanged addresses and phone numbers, and the idea was to meet up at their place a few days later. My pals all shook my hand, then shook their heads, hoping something similar would happen to them if they kept waving champagne bottles and smiled enough.

Inside the club was an enormous fountain, spraying brilliant jets of water 20 feet into the air. It was quite a spectacle, and was an intrinsic part of the atmosphere of this inimitable club. Through the sprays of the fountain I was watching a topless geezer with his hands in the air, screaming at the top of his voice. When the water stopped I recognised the raver as a bloke named Dave Fix It. He was so tagged because he could fix literally anything. He was about 40, married with three kids and a car mechanic's business in Essex. But all of that must have seemed a long way away, as he was savouring the ecstasy of this moment, going mental and completely oblivious to my beckoning shouts. I wasn't about to get wet, so I left Fix It to his merry buzz.

The hours flew by. By 8 a.m., as usual, our motley crew were the last people standing and amongst the only ones left in the club. We'd ended up on the VIP balcony next to the DJ console, where the vinyl technician played just for us. It felt like being royalty, although much more Prince Charlie than any old Queen Mother.

I suppose you could say things had got slightly out of hand. I mean, the abusive way we treated our bodies could – and would – have serious implications later in life. It wasn't that any of us had a death-wish; it was just a case of living for the moment. Dominic produced a bag of trips he'd purchased earlier and handed them round the balcony.

'Can I interest one in a tab of LSD, madam?' I heard him say to a Spanish woman collecting glasses. Amanda told the VIPs the party would continue for a couple of extra hours, and then everyone would be invited to the after-party at a nearby villa. Amanda was a lovely girl, a living (usually), breathing symbol of Girl Power. Being articulate and organised, no matter how messy she got or how many days she'd been awake, business was always top of her agenda. Still, once that was taken care of, she'd hit the dance floor like a natural-born groover. As Amanda busted her moves, the 50 or so people left in the club made enough noise for over a hundred. Our screams of joy echoed and bounced around the enormous empty nightclub, as the sun burst from high in the sky and filled the whole building with gorgeous golden rays.

Everybody was well and truly tripping as Jock took a load of orders and went off somewhere to score a trunkful of drugs. The VIP balcony overlooking the dance floor had a solid glass floor. Soon enough, Dominic and Tank – completely off their trolleys – were wrestling on the floor until they knocked over a table, sending its glass surface shattering on the dance floor, and the sound of breaking glass resounding through the club.

Patting one another down, the terrible twosome rose to their feet and necked half a bottle of champers each. I was with Windross, rolling a joint, when the closely cropped Danny NF (who hated being called that, because he was certainly no racist) came along with a tray of drinks and stepped straight on to the broken glass. Thinking the floor was breaking under his feet, he threw the tray in the air and grunted awkwardly as his legs bent at the knees. The tray whizzed over everyone's heads and crashed 30 feet to the concrete floor below. The after-shock was silence. Everybody stood staring at Danny, while Tank and Dominic were doubled up in pain from laughing so much.

It was at about this time that Amanda announced the DJ was playing his last record and read out the address of the after-party. Several of our posse went straight there, whilst Ed and I went to find Jock, who by this point had been gone for several hours. He lived in the hills behind San Antonio in a very residential area, so we drove around the winding roads until we were confronted by the heart-churning sight of Jock's English-registered vehicle, completely burnt out. Our buzz immediately disappeared. Everything on the car, including the tyres, was burnt to a shell.

As we carried on up the hill, our concerns grew even greater as we tried to find our mate. We banged on his door loudly and, in a panic, our shouts drowned out the replies that were gradually emerging. As soon as we saw he was OK, our excitement at seeing our buddy almost suffocated us, and we all hugged each other passionately. Jock lined the gear up before telling us his story.

'Mate, you ain't ever gonna believe what's happened ta me,' were his first, ominous words.

As Jock told it, he'd come out of Ku completely off his tits.

'I dunno how I drove back,' he continued. 'I got halfway up the hill, when I could smell smoke. I stopped the fucking car to see what's up and all this smoke came up from the dashboard! My driver's door couldnae open right, so I climbed outta me seat and leapt through the open passenger window. By the time I got to mer feet, the car was in a ball of flames, man!'

Jock told us that the flames from the car were burning a nearby tree!

'I couldnae believe it,' he splurted. 'I had all the fucking drugs in me boxers, I'm coked up and tripping, and the next thang I know all these sirens are going off around me!'

The local coppers had arrived within minutes, shouting in Spanish and trying desperately to put the fire out with extinguishers. Suddenly about 30 Guardia had shown up and had helicopters flying over the burning trees. One of them, according to Jock, spoke a bit of English. He'd explained that the officers might have to evacuate the whole area because of the smouldering trees.

'The fire brigade couldnae get up the hill because of the coppers' cars,' spluttered Jocky. 'When they got through, it only took five minutes to put the flames out. But me car was completely burnt out, man! I was standing there with this copper, shatting meself; I thought they were gonna take me to the station. But after they got me name and put the fire out, the Pigs left me standing there with about 60 Spanish neighbours. I went back tar me place and cleaned it out, in case the Guardia came back. That was about half an hour ago, and I'm still buzzing, mate!'

We laughed, then did some more gear before heading for the after-party. We found the villa easily enough, but everyone was standing outside. It turned out that Amanda and her team hadn't shown up yet, so no one could get into the villa. There were people already inside who claimed they didn't have the key and that the after-party wasn't being held there, anyway. Unsurprisingly, the crowd of over a hundred didn't believe them and refused to go away, singing and dancing in the small, congested road.

Around the building was a high wall. It wasn't difficult to scale: once on top you only had to step from the wall on to the roof. A couple of guys helped some girls climb on to the roof, until there wasn't enough room for anyone else. Some nutter then took a running jump off the roof into the swimming pool. Soaking wet, he ignored the occupants' pleas and found a ladder long enough for them to climb down from one roof in single file. Once on ground level, the search for music and excess booze commenced and abruptly ended with two bottles of San Miguel. This wasn't a good sign. Suddenly the guy who was actually staying at the villa pulled up and said that the party was somewhere else. Slightly pissed off, we decided to go to Mambo's.

By 4 p.m. our posse of PaPAs (Pathetic Party Animals!) had caned every bottle of schnapps in the gaff. Jason Bye-Bye played heaps of classic hip-hop, soul and house tracks. Encouraging other drinkers to sing along, about a hundred of us sang loads of De La Soul. Taking it a step further, we ended up having a grand-scale dancing competition, before caning it up at the Havin' It villa until just after 2 a.m.

The moral of this story is that there are crap nights in Ibiza, but on a scale of UK crappiness, even the crap ones are pretty special. And don't forget, I still had those dancers' phone numbers!

# **13** The Delay

'One for the road' is probably one of the most widely used metaphors on the island, especially when it comes to the end of the holiday and you're supposed to be at the villa, packing your shit together. Johnny Tourist, ever eager, is always the first to reach the airport and stand patiently in line waiting to offload his luggage. You can always spot a Johnny. Skin burnt to a cinder, he's always – always! – wearing a football shirt or a filthy T-shirt with some shitty bar's slogan across his chest, relating how many drinks his mates have knocked back. Other essential Johnny accoutrements are Levi's jeans, Ralph Lauren shirt, baseball cap with curved peak and the *de rigueur* crap trainers. Johnny Tourists always annoy their fellow-travellers by being loud, abusive, obnoxious and an embarrassment to themselves and anyone else in the area. But do they care? Nah, and why should they! Life is for living, innit? So that's just what they do – if at times the living of it can be decidedly uncomfortable.

Johnny Tourist's idea of a good night is to get completely thrashed and try to grab hold of any girl who cares to walk past him. If that's his thing, let 'im get on with it. I'm not one for making judgements on other people's lifestyles. I know, there are enough people lining up to judge me on my own lifestyle.

Whatever way you look at it, Ibiza veterans won't go anywhere near the airport until half an hour before take-off. In the early days they used to sit moodily drinking beers from the terminal's cafeteria for hour after hour. But nowadays the vets time it just right, arriving long after Johnny Tourist has checked in, so that the terminal is more or less empty.

Unfortunately that wasn't going to happen one day in '96.

The airport was full to capacity and was experiencing long-term delays due to an air-traffic controllers' strike. To make matters worse, the airline staff were pushed beyond all limits, battling with frustrated Johnny Tourists, and didn't have a clue when normal services would resume.

The official line was that the authorities expected travellers to hang out in the terminal, awaiting further instructions. The unofficial line was that this was total bollocks. Jay, Eric, Dan, Nikki, Pip and I held our ground as we checked in our cases, while a few of the other mob went back into Ibiza Town in search of something to eat.

It took three hours to rid our crew of our luggage. Three bleedin' hours! The only things to do in an airport are shop, drink, drink, shop, and then get completely blasted. The news of our plane – delayed for an 'undisclosed' period – really upset us, especially since we'd left a load of our pals having a wicked time at KM5. We'd been in Space all day before the entourage moved on to that bar, which was situated on a lonely road between San Ann and the airport. It was a fairly small bar, but had a massive garden, with various stage props plotted here and there. Noise pollution wasn't a problem, because it was isolated from neighbouring houses and stores. We could scream, shout and sing to our hearts' content. Wicked!

I'd met some good pals in Space, and we'd all been sitting around a table talking about our love of life. One girl in particular paid me a lot of attention. She said she came from Notting Hill, and she looked Italian. She'd been sorta following me around for ages, but I hadn't really taken much notice. Too much else was going on. Soon enough, though, the Woody Woodpecker started to take effect and I felt like I was gonna be sick. I managed to find a quiet, shed-like structure just outside the garden boundaries and sat down in anticipation of regurgitating the Es mashed up in my stomach. The sun hadn't gone down yet, so it was still light outside. Suddenly my Number One Fan appeared out of the bushes, walking into an area where she thought she couldn't be seen by anyone. Before I knew it, she was pulling down her knickers and taking a leak. I couldn't help laughing quietly, but really I wondered if she knew I was there. Suddenly she looked around to see me watching her.

She finished and wandered over.

'Are you OK?'

My guts were playing havoc with my senses, and I figured that being seen as an out-of-it, puking pee-watcher would do my reputation no good. Still, she didn't seem to mind or even notice, but out of respect for both of us I asked her to leave me alone for a while, so I could pull myself together. Typically, within minutes all of 20 people had converged in the shed!

The boys' antidote for feeling rough – so they delightedly told me – was to inhale South American snowflakes. Wow! Bloody weird, but they were right. Within minutes I was back on form and ready to continue the mad-for-it orgy of drugs, mental illness and a not inconsiderable amount of alcohol.

Suddenly, though, as we stepped out from the shed, the cries of Old Bill came over the garden. Oh shit! Three jeeploads of Guardia were parked outfront and facing the group. The doors opened and out they came, Ibiza's own Old Bill. The boys were all searched, but luckily most of us had already ditched or sniffed our stash. When the coast was finally clear, the goods were retrieved and put to good use. Ahem!

I loitered in the car park, changing from a sarong into my London clothes (warm jumper, jeans, boots, slightly more furrowed eyebrows) as my new Italian friend announced that she had something to tell me. I thought – not unreasonably, given recent events – that she was taking the piss. Especially when she went on to discuss her love of intellectual men. This is Wayne Anthony, for Pete's sake! I may be many things, and I definitely am some of them, but intellectual? Well, maybe after a few tabs.

Nevertheless, she went for gold and stuck her tongue right down my throat.

I told her there was no way we could go any further unless she was gonna give it over. Me, get all worked up to end it with a kiss and cuddle? Those days are up. If it was romance she wanted, why didn't she go on holiday to Paris, Venice or Stratford-on-bleedin'-Avon? She wasn't too amused by this at all, and explained that she was a 'nice girl' and that she preferred to get to know someone before they ripped her knickers off. I mean, all well and good, but I was due to be on a plane in less than two hours.

Funnily enough, I didn't really fancy knocking one out in the bogs, so bare-facedly I turned her down. I hoped she understood my angle, but wasn't completely sure. We were all gutted at having to leave on such a high – everyone had been really enjoying themselves. Djeck, Jarvis (Biology), Windross, Alan (Vibe), Jenny, Ann, Smudge and Siri took the piss out of our group for flying back to wet and dreary London. We waved goodbye to our supposedly good friends and reluctantly hit the road. The rest, of course, was history.

The news arrived that we wouldn't be able to board the plane for at least another couple of hours. I was dying for a kip and some people were crashing out on the rows of plastic seats and on the concrete, which by all accounts was marginally more comfortable. It looked like a huge bomb shelter, as bodies littered the floor. Parts of the airport were shut down for the night, leaving an eerie silence, as if we were in some kind of modern war. As I was kipping I was rudely awoken by the loud and cheerful James, who'd just arrived from the old town. The lucky git had just eaten a three-course meal washed down with five or six bottles of plonk.

'Oi, Wayne, you nutter!' he yelled. 'The plane's gonna be delayed for another three hours so I've brought some quiver to keep us going.'

Quiver? Oh fuck! I wanted to get some sleep.

Truth be told, there didn't seem much point in sleeping. The guys had built a great camp in the terminal by moving rows of seats into a courtyard shape. James woke everyone up, telling them the good and bad news. Then he huddled into his throne, as he piled the powder on the backs of at least fifteen hands. Everybody chipped in and gave him the money he'd paid for the half-ounce of Charlie.

'You taking that back with you?' asked DJ Pants (aka Steve Friend), who'd never taken drugs in his life.

'You gotta be joking. We're doing this before we leave, mate,' laughed Eric. Jay was the only person James couldn't wake, which wasn't surprising because he and his girlfriend Nikki took turns at sleeping for England. Seriously, if there was a sport that involved sleeping, Darren, Jay and Nikki would be world champions. Even Sleeping Beauty would have her work cut out if she came across this trio of sleeping uglies! Jay sprawled out on the floor snoring like a good 'un. Everyone tried different anti-snoring remedies, which failed miserably. The thing with Jay is, if he's not on drugs he sleeps lightly and can be easily woken, but when he's been on it, the job's a bad one. Someone suggested piling quiver just below his nose, so the next time he inhaled he'd be Charlied. It worked. The tiny white crystals went straight to his brain and woke the startled Jay in seconds.

'Jesus fucking Christ!'

Oddly enough, he wasn't too pleased!

We'd now been in the airport for just over twelve hours. The airport staff began handing out food vouchers to everyone waiting to travel, but a free sandwich and one drink were hardly a top freebie, so we chucked them. To make things that bit more frustrating, the airline – which I can't name for legal reasons, the gits – hadn't a clue when the plane would be cleared to leave, but kept promising us that the problem would be resolved and back to normal at any time. What a load of shit!

An hour or more later our plane was finally ready to board. Everyone sat exactly where they wanted on the plane, which it turned out wasn't even owned by the airline we'd originally booked with. To reassure us, the cabin crew didn't look too keen on the emergency arrangements made by both companies. In fact, they had the right hump! It wasn't our fault; we should have been well home and kipping by the time this plane touched down in Ibiza. In the time we'd been stuck in the airport, we could have flown to England and back four times, read *War and Peace* or even *Mixmag*, and translated one of Arsene Wenger's press conferences at Arsenal. As far as I saw it, we had every right to be pissed off: a little bit, at least.

We sat at the back of the plane. Clunk-click. With the engines purring, the aircraft sat on the runway for over half an hour . . . then the engines went off. For fuck's sake! One of the flight attendants glared at me, with absolutely no sign of emotion.

'Can I have a drink while we're waiting to take off?' I implored.

No response. Then she looked at me in disgust and walked away without even acknowledging my request. Everyone started laughing at the look on my face as I sat amazed at her abruptness. As she reappeared, I demanded a drink. It wasn't as if I wanted alcohol. I only asked for a soft juice.

'There isn't any food or drink on the plane,' she lied profusely, before informing me that the aircraft was chartered to fly somewhere else, before an emergency re-schedule to Manchester.

'Manchester? Mad for it! Fookin top one MANCHEST-AH?'

Everyone was outraged, because the plane was supposed to fly to Gatwick. That was the last straw.

'Right, we want to get off!' I shouted at the flight attendant.

'You can't get off.'

'Yes, we can – and we are – so you'd better do whatever you got to to get our suitcases off this plane. If you think we're gonna sit here and put up with your ignorant attitude, you're way wrong. I want my cases, and I want them now!'

The others were clapping and cheering my outraged speech, as tears formed in the flight attendant's eyes. She ran off. I think she was actually crying (just think, I could have been there before Ian Brown!).

Just as we were preparing to gatecrash the runway, the stewardess confidently reappeared with the captain, the co-pilots and what must have been the entire crew.

'Ladies and gentlemen, please calm down,' blathered Captain Mouthwash. 'I'm really sorry for the delay. I'm waiting for traffic control to clear us for take-off. It should be any time now. Please sit down in your allocated seats and I'll check with Control to see if we can go in the next 20 minutes.'

This was about as pacifying as a red rag dipped in bull's blood to a gaping-nostrilled black beast who'd just been told his own 'old cow' indoors had been served up for a matadorial breakfast.

'No, you don't understand. We booked these flights to and from Gatwick,' I raged. 'There's obviously been some mix-up with the flight numbers, because we're not going to Manchester!'

Mouthwash gave it his best shot.

'OK, let me explain. The airline you booked with hasn't got

any more flights leaving this airport until Wednesday. Because of the air controllers' strike there's nothing anyone can do. I'm very sorry the situation wasn't explained to you earlier. If you fly with us to Manchester, I'm sure the airline has contingency plans for you all.'

Yeah, and I could see it now: a clapped-out World War I biplane piloted by Bez!

'This is outrageous! What about the food and drink situation?' asked a flabbergasted Pants.

The cabin crew blathered on about us having been given emergency vouchers at the airport, and insisted that if we weren't in the air within 20 minutes, we'd be allowed to leave the plane.

'Just so everybody knows, we are quite within our rights to demand that he let us off the plane and return our luggage, before the plane can leave the runway,' said James.

'Yes, you do have that right, but first let me do what I said I'd do and get us in the air,' pleaded Cap'n Mouthwash.

All right, that seemed fairly reasonable. Off he went, and order was restored once more, and the engines were started . . . after nineteen minutes! Typically, it was at least another 20 before we reached the sky.

At Manchester airport, the passengers couldn't wait to get hold of someone from the airline, but when we reached the baggage hall there were no brass bands, no dancing girls and, most obviously, no flight attendants.

Somebody started singing, sarcastically, 'I wish they all could be California girls . . .'

None of that, mate.

James and his lot booked into a nearby hotel and a flight to Gatwick for later that night. The airline's representatives, bearing the brunt of it all, arranged for coaches to take an entire planeful of passengers to London. Jay, Bubbles, Eric, Dan, Pip and I refused point-blank to go anywhere near the coaches. We were determined that our complaints would be heard. Finally a stewardess came out and did sympathise with us. But there was no point screaming or shouting at her – she'd only just started her shift.

We went out to the main terminal and sat down to breakfast at McDonald's. No sooner had we sat down than one of the other stewardesses, who'd greeted us when we landed, asked us if we wanted a coach to ourselves. She said the driver would take us to Gatwick or drop us somewhere on the way. It was an offer that, under the circumstances, couldn't be refused. There was lots of room on the coach, curtains that could be drawn and an on-board stereo. A deal was struck with the driver, who agreed to make several stops on the way: Hemel Hempstead via Milton Keynes, where I and a few others got off at the BP petrol station. We called a cab and were soon home, after a mind-boggling 26-hour journey from the time we first entered the Spanish airport. We could have flown to Australia in less time and suffered the same jetlag ... In case anyone forgets to tell you, sometimes going to Ibiza is just like visiting hell.

# **14** Wet Dreams

Time passed quickly, considering I'd been awake for three days, but I could feel the tiredness encroaching on my dwindling supplies of energy. The ravers' express train had come to a halt at Alfie's place. Alfie was born in London, but had lived in Los Angeles for fifteen years. There was a whole bunch of people at his apartment, including his brother Joe, Gabby, Diana, Hilda and Jo, who all lived in Australia.

The tiredness did its grand finale and the Fat Lady stripped to her G-string. I fell into an exhausted trance state, totally cabbaged. Or so I thought.

I woke suddenly to find myself lying on a giant round bed. Standing solitarily upright in the middle of the huge round room was a single white door, with an exaggerated brass door handle. I shook my head several times in disbelief, trying to remove the cobwebs in my mind, formed over the past 76 hours. But, hypnotised by the doorway's mystic properties, I cautiously approached and turned the handle. A warm, bright light engulfed the room, and for a brief moment I thought back to certain TV programmes about paranormal phenomena that I'd seen. When people spoke about near-death experiences, they always talked of a brilliant light, which they perceived as being good. I may not have been dead or even dying, but I decided to step through the doorway.

Immediately I found myself standing on a narrow marble pathway perched high above a grand canyon. The sky was split into night and day. On my right side was night-time, as two full moons and a galaxy of stars sparkled against a pitch-black backdrop. On my left, a beautiful hot day, with four different suns emitting ultra-violet rays on to the red canyon below.

Another alluring doorway stood temptingly at the path's end, just over 200 yards away. I made my way towards the door, admiring the wonderful view.

I could see something gliding over the sun-drenched mountains, and as it moved closer the flying figure took on the shape of an American Indian bald eagle. I gazed admiringly at the giant predator now circling a lake at the bottom of the valley. The eagle went into a dive towards the shining water and disappeared from view, but seconds later the bird reappeared with a fish five times its size locked in its sharp claws, wriggling and trying to escape its hungry clutches. The bird flew right past me, creating a back-draught of wind that should have sent me tumbling down into the canyon, but a cushion of air stopped me from falling over the edge and held me in place. I watched as the eagle disappeared into the moonlit mountains.

I turned the brass handle and opened the next door. Inside was a prehistoric rainforest, with trees, plant and animal life-forms like I'd never seen before. The tall green trees reached up to the skies to re-create a green stairway to the heavens. The unusual plants and flowers were brightly coloured in purple, red, blue, orange and yellow. The forest teemed with life, but the strange silence of the woods was broken by the sound of water falling. I began to explore the surrounding area for the source of the mesmerising noise. Homing in on the sound, before long I found an opening in some trees. I stepped on to a ledge at the top of a breathtaking waterfall. At the bottom was a large, white grand piano, and on top of the piano was a woman, twisting and turning as the water gently pounded her naked body. She looked up at me with dark beautiful eyes, although her lips didn't move. I heard a female voice inside my head.

'Orion said you would come.'

My clothes came off in seconds and I dived into the clear blue water. Beneath the surface were thousands of fish: I was completely surrounded by an array of colour and movement. Their tiny bodies gently touched my skin until they all seemed to vanish at once. There in front of me was the woman. Intuitively I held out my hand and pulled her closer to me. We began to glide through the water as my mouth touched hers, our hands caressing one another's bodies.

Out of the deep blue shadows a dolphin swam towards us. The large mammal playfully searched around us, nudging my hand on to its fin and gracefully pulling us through the water. A magnificent underwater city came into view: one of the buildings stood out from the others and could quite easily be a palace of some sort. The city's round, domed roofs were lined with gold, silver and glass. The dolphin left us standing on a platform in front of the palace's huge gates. It was so real. Was I really dreaming?

My companion turned the handle on the gate. Beyond the barrier was a vast desert: we stepped out of the water on to the warm sand. Several planets in a straight line created a spectacular sky view. A lagoon surrounded by palm trees lay just ahead, so we ran and jumped into its refreshing, cooling water. Taking her in my arms, again I began kissing and caressing her. Despite the fact that I felt safe from harm, my sixth sense told me we were being closely watched, and that every move we were making was almost being manipulated by some unseen entity.

Suddenly we were startled by the sound of a horse, and we looked up to see a majestic white unicorn. We climbed out of the water and on to its back, whereupon it began running towards a sand dune and down the other side, where a whole herd of multicoloured unicorns was drinking from a huge aluminium dish that was levitating above the sand. The herd joined us and ran by our side, moving rapidly, whilst everything else seemed in slow motion. In the distance we could see three bright stars closely grouped together, each more dazzling than anything else in the sky and changing colour from red and blue to silver and green.

The unicorns ran faster and faster towards the constellation. As it turned out, the three 'stars' were in fact the tips of three grandiose red pyramids, and as we got closer to the Egyptian monuments we could see thousands of people in flowing white gowns standing on the steps. They had large silver horns in their hands and were playing a fanfare, which echoed loudly for miles around. Five manned ancient Egyptian ships floated 60 feet above floor-level to the right of the biggest pyramid. A passageway opened in one of the large steps: on either side of the entrance were roaring lions mounted on columns with hieroglyphics carved into the limestone (they looked like the sort of gibberish I used to write when I'd had too many Es)!

Anyway, the herd of unicorns slowed to a halt, as our animal ran straight into a dark corridor. This was nothing to do with the drugs, you understand, but large images formed around us, depicting historical monuments, various visuals of mankind, a Mandingo warrior, pharaohs, star alignments, an hourglass, images of my past and possibly of my future. The unicorn came to a halt in front of a powerful, blue electric force-field, which made a strong humming noise. We dismounted and the unicorn turned and galloped back down the corridor. I reached out to touch the electric field, watching my hand completely disappear into the mystical barrier. The electricity stimulated my mind and body, and my inner spirit felt rejuvenated by this tingling sensation. It was, I confess, not totally unlike someone whacking your funny bone with a blunt object, except this was much more pleasant.

Sticking my scrambled head through the mystical phenomena, I could see the rainforest . . . and hey, no Sting! Instead I wanted the woman to feel the revitalising energy I received from the field, so I offered her the light. We began to levitate slowly four feet above the ground, our physical beings exchanging electrical charges. As we snogged, the blue energy bursts intensified and she wrapped her legs around me. We closed our eyes and felt our consciousness sailing through the air at great speed, towards what I can only describe as the best narcotic or sexual climax I've had in my entire life! It was as if the entire planet earth, the universe and evolution itself were within our understanding. We viewed the galaxy and its entire contents through the eyes of a creator – not the sort of thing I normally come up with as pillow talk, I can tell ya!

We watched the gods engaged in a battle for the cosmos before gasping at the sight of a giant blue whale skimming between nebulas. The kings and kings of kings were astounded by the unannounced spectator and laid down their weapons to behold one another. The warm-blooded mammal disappeared into a sheet of darkness. We followed suit, and jumped into the same black hole, landing on the floor of the prehistoric jungle, just yards from the waterfall where we first met.

Who is this woman? I thought. Does she get to Romford?

A voice in my head spoke: 'My name is Cleopatra. You are from the new world . . . I have waited many suns and moons. Orion said you would come.'

She dived into the water and I followed, but I'd lost her. Emerging, I found a beach, but no Cleo. I felt afraid, and totally vacant, when out of the bush came the unicorn. Reassured, I got on the horse's back and it ran through the sand in the direction of a small, round hut at the opposite end of the beach. As I prepared to enter the bamboo structure, I stopped to thank the unicorn for its guidance. There was something very familiar about the horse – looking into the beast's eyes felt as if I were seeing my own soul. My inner thoughts told me the unicorn represented my own energies; the horse was a part of my total being. My soul seemed to fill with energy; my neurological activity increased and became charged with light. I stepped into the hut.

I found myself in a large, circular room with one of the white doorways propped in the centre. On the wall were neanderthal drawings depicting different prehistoric rituals. I turned the handle and entered the star-gate, and in a flash I was back in the bedroom. There was a figure in my bed. It was Cleopatra: she gave a beautiful smile. A soft, soothing voice inside my head said: 'I have dreamt of a man with your likeness. I have waited many suns and moons.'

Nice work if I could get it!

I heard the roar of big cats, and by the entrance to the apartment stood the lions from the pyramid. I asked Cleo if I was dreaming, and she told me to close my eyes, whereupon I could feel myself being dramatically shaken, before hearing my name called. As I opened my eyes, a bright flash left me temporarily blinded. When my blurred vision returned to normal, there was a mirror in front of me. I saw what I thought was my own reflection, but someone had put a blond pigtailed wig on my head, my eyebrows were shaved off, and I was wearing hooker-red lipstick around my face. Cold baked beans trickled down the front of my trousers and I wore a woman's bra . . . This was an even more frightening sight than the flippin' lions!

I snapped out of a trance to find one of the girls standing over me with a camera and about ten others rolling about on the floor. They were just laughing; they were pissing themselves so much I'm amazed one of them didn't have a coronary. I couldn't decide which was worse: the lipstick, the bra or the beans! I wrestled with the photographer. Sadly, the lads overpowered me and I could do nothing to prevent the film being immediately taken out of the house and hidden somewhere. It was developed the next day and handed out as flyers in Mambo's and the Rock Bar, where I'm sure everybody had a bloody good laugh, even if I didn't exactly hurry back there to join them. But Cleopatra, Orion and Egypt, well that's another story.

I'm sure I've had more embarrassing experiences, but if you think I'm gonna tell you about those, you're even madder than I am.

Now, where did I park that unicorn?

# **15** Late Arrivals

If someone promises to pick you up at Evissa aiport, don't flippin' count on it. In fact, newcomers have about as much chance of being met at Arrivals in Ibiza as finding life on Mars. They would be much better off catching a taxi straight to the villa, or even one of the bars where everyone hangs out. The problem is: things are done differently here. You've heard of Greenwich Mean Time – well, Ibiza should have Spanish Meanie Time, in honour of a particularly potent form of psychedelics. It's not just that Ibiza has a time difference, but everyone is on a completely different astral plane, as well as buckets of pharmaceuticals. Schedules are rearranged on a daily basis, because no one can foresee what's gonna happen next, except that it's gonna be mad. Why? Because it always was.

We'd been out of it since Space early that morning. I wasn't just tired, I was completely fuckin' thrashed. My intoxicated body just wanted to curl up into a ball and sleep, but if I didn't get to the airport on time to meet my friends, they would start bawling. There was no way I could get out of it: the responsibility of looking for a suitable villa had been left down to me, and the only things I let down are balloons and my own trousers. The villa was hidden up in the mountains and would be fairly complicated to find, if you didn't know the signs to look for. If it was a bunch of lads, I wouldn't have been as concerned, but I was looking after a very good mate with his long-term girlfriend and a couple of her buddies. Which meant a major falling out if I left them standing in the terminal.

The problem wasn't the driving: oh no, my main problem was just staying awake! Teasingly, I had a fair old notion that if I went to collect the group and the plane was delayed, there was a very good chance I could crash out on a bench somewhere. A mouldy old plastic seat had never seemed more attractive. On the other hand, I ran the risk of not being seen, which might lead my pals to conclude I wasn't coming. If we missed each other at the airport, the result would have been big potatoes.

Nevertheless, I was fucked – really, really fucked – and so was everyone else. I decided to leave Zenith, because the longer I stayed there, the more drunk I was getting. Zenith was a beach bar, a nice place comprising a small marquee top, varnished wooden floors, sound system, decks, bar, lights, tables and some snazzy designer chairs. The bar really kicked into gear after Space had closed on Sunday evenings. Hundreds of people would head straight there, eager to continue the party. Situated on a beach, backdropped by mountains and sea, Zenith seemed to have sprung out of nowhere. One minute it wasn't there, the next it was. Ravers could dance to the sounds of DJs Pippi and Ellis, or just sit back, chill out and take in the amazing surroundings.

It was only 7 p.m. so the sun hadn't yet set. The light of day revealed some interesting, very odd-looking characters. Some were dressed outlandishly, others more conservatively, but all were totally high. I must admit, sometimes it can be quite a buzz in itself just watching the effects of Ecstasy. The facial expressions can be a living theatre on their own. I stood at the bar at Zenith, watching the multitude of faces being pulled apart by the tablet's influence: jawbones shattering together, pupils bursting out of their sockets and the overall effect like watching those Victorian places they christened Bedlam (that's the nutty house to you and me). It wasn't just one or two people – there was a ratio of at least a 40 per cent feverish tongue-twisters to the other 60 per cent who were trying desperately to look like anything except the barmy people around them.

I still had a few hours to get to the airport, so I decided it might be best to get on the move and try to stay awake. I suppose I could have had a two-hour power-nap and felt as right as rain, but then again I could easily have collapsed into a two-day coma! If I fell asleep now, that might be it.

## Spanish Highs

I drove Sally and Joanna to their apartment in San Ann. In the entire eight weeks I'd been on the island I'd never once had to ask someone else to drive my car. But Joanna seemingly came to my rescue by suggesting that she drove – which, looking back, was the most sensible course of action. But then I wasn't looking back. I was there, and I was mad.

I lasted two minutes before I changed my mind and got back into the driver's seat. After failing to persuade the girls to collect my friends from the airport, I remembered the one person who might be able to help me: Neil Armstrong! Naw, not the flippin' astronaut. The other one – the space cadet!

Neil lived in the old town, where a lot of the Spanish gypsies lived. He was a good mate from England, who was staying with his Spanish girlfriend and some French girl. The winding roads were very narrow in places, with enough room for just one car at a time, but I somehow managed to negotiate them until I reached Neil's place. There were a few cars parked along the wall, so I tucked the vehicle right up against it with the others and got out from the passenger side. As I did so, a battered old car came up the hill and started honking its horn at me. Who was this fucking maniac? There was easily enough room for the car to get through, but the driver – some banana in his late forties – became very angry and started shouting in Spanish.

He stopped in the middle of the road and ripped the seatbelt from its buckle. He then came charging at me, totally enraged. I couldn't believe how angry the guy was: he didn't give a fuck. The man practically chased me around the narrow road hurling some serious abuse. I swore at him in Italian, and Maltese, which enraged him even more. He put a hand in his jacket pocket and pulled out a fuckin' knife. He swung the knife around like a madman and wasn't at all concerned if the blade collided with my weary flesh. One false move and it was stitches – if not curtains. The game was over. As soon as he came within range, I smacked him on the nose, before running to my friend's house. Pushing open the door (which was ajar), I ran up the stairs, past Neil and into the kitchen. Behind me, the crazy fucking knifeman was coming up the stairs screaming and shouting. As I searched for a weapon, Neil begged me to stay put whilst he sorted it out. Armstrong went to the top of the stairs, where he could see the man, and walked down towards him. Moments later the shouting had stopped and Neil returned with news of the Old Bill being on their way.

I wasn't gonna stand around waiting to be arrested: I'd only wanted Neil to pick the others up! I didn't need any of this, especially not just after leaving an environment where people were riddled with drugs and were supposed to be properly psychotic! Here, in the aged silence of this very old town, an addled pensioner was trying to kill or maim a happy clubber!

The Guardia's arrival was imminent, so I had to escape before they got there. Peeping through the window out front, I could see a crowd of people standing with the old bloke. From where I was, it looked just like a lynch mob. I ran into the street, screaming at the group, and made a bolt for the car. But they collared me and immediately pinned me to the bonnet, shouting in Spanish – and I don't think they were offering me *paella*. Fearing that I could be stabbed at any time, I somehow conjured up a hidden force – probably a combination of fatigue-induced adrenaline and sheer, splenetic rage – which threw my attackers off, and fled on foot. Luckily, I managed to make it down to the safety of the Rock Bar, where I changed clothes with a friend. Someone proffered a wrap of coke, which I sniffed at once. That certainly woke me up. Perhaps, finally, my plans would come to fruition.

I called the airport to see if it was possible to leave a message for the arriving party. However, the information desk told me – with, I'm sure, a smidgen of palpable delight – that the plane was being delayed until the following day. The day's events flashed through my mind as I contemplated this knowledge and the phone crashed to the floor. Twelve hours without sleep, lots of mental grief and an octogenarian knifeman! The worst thing was, I was now so totally wired on Charlie that I wasn't able to sleep for the next twelve hours. Finally I totally collapsed, didn't make it to the airport and had a massive bleedin' ding-dong row anyway!

Oi, old fella, sorry about that!

# 16 The Havin' It Villa

Ibiza's pumping club scene is equally matched by its private party circuit. Experienced veterans rent their own self-contained villas, so that when the clubs finish, everyone can pile back to their places for the exclusive after-parties. During the summer of 1995, Casa Galiano was renamed the Havin' It villa: I don't think you need me to tell you why!

The Spanish house had been rented for the summer by myself and a friend and had four bedrooms, two kitchens, a balcony area, huge lounge and a swimming pool, surrounded by a spacious concrete-finished garden. Well nice!

Most of the time, I was hanging out with my friend Ed, another big-time party animal with time to spare and money to burn. We knew all the important faces in Ibiza and were well respected as old-school party promoters: it was hard to avoid a fun and sniff-filled atmosphere whenever we were around. We were stupid, bananas and cauliflowers, mad-for-it big boys!

After 'Love It' at Pacha on Monday mornings, a selection of invited guests would usually make their way to the Canin' ... sorry, Havin' It villa. That morning was more or less the same as all the other mad parties. There were bodies scattered all round the place, top DJs on the decks and lots of disco dust in carefully situated little stashes. Out on the porch it was like King Arthur and the Knights of the Round Tablet. This was where deranged discussion of the theories of evolution and other confused ramblings would take place. Einstein was labelled a bullshitter way ahead of his time. Darwin's natural selection was pulverised. Newton was branded another trick-ster ... Also, according to the sniffed-up logic, the pyramids were built using ancient magic; Stonehenge was some kind of porthole to another world; pills from California were better than those from Holland; garage music was better than drum 'n' bass; Sean Connery's James Bond was pure class; and there were other similar, stoned claims, such as the location of the best Ibiza sunset, the most favoured nightclub (Pacha), how Latino señoritas are way beyond stunning and, most ridiculous of all, that I was quite a normal geezer, really. I'm sure you get the drift . . .

Anyway, for some daft reason, a flurry of stories about crazy fishing trips was sparked off by someone going on about a girl who'd slipped out of their net. The one that got away, and all that bollocks. Well, as you may be gathering, I can tell a story or two and somehow I got to telling the tale about the time I went shark-fishing, with a hired yacht, captain, a full crew and, most obviously, the prerequisite 'gear'.

And we're not talking sou'westers!

We left the girls at the villa and went in search of a huge shark or, better still, a great white bite to eat. If it came to the top, the captain didn't know it, but we'd already planned to blast it with his hunting shotgun. It was 6 a.m., the sun was rising on the horizon, seagulls were having feeding frenzies, and we were ready to go. We were stocked up with puff, crates of champagne, and one pill each. The nearest land was 25 miles away and the water was as smooth as my moves on the dance floor . . . er, read into that what you will!

Anyway, the captain took us to a spot in the middle of fucking nowhere and said it was *the* place to catch the biggest sharks. The stereo blasted an old Mickey Finn tape, so we were dancing around the boat waving our arms about like nutters. They called the bait 'chum' and I soon found out why – it smelt even worse than a glue factory. The absolute pits. It consisted of (wait for it) animal guts, fish pieces, untold blood and all kinds of other crap. Lovely? Nah, not really. But to a man-eating shark it was like an *à la carte* meal.

They were clever blighters, the sharks, and quick too. A sonar (or summat!)-guided fish can pinpoint and home in on its prey from over 2,000 feet away. Before you can yell 'Shark!', it'll have your leg off and be washing it down with a mouthful of salt. Warily, we lowered the shit into the water in steel buckets, which let the pieces of bait float out gradually, like a greasy cocktail of stale death.

Six badly maintained fishing rods were placed around the stern. We had these massive hooks on-line and cast our man-made traps. Totally prepared to battle a great white and bring the trophy home for our girlfriends, we were. My buddies Weasel and Touch came from a tough neck of the woods: they weren't scared of anything. Together, we kept on dancing whilst keeping a close eye on our floats. I took a moment to absorb the surrounding area. Clouds formed beautiful patterns across the rising morning sun, which bleached the deep blue with crystals of light. A microscopic dot in the sea represented our boat. Gorgeous, it was.

A few hours passed with no sign of a shark attack, so we suggested throwing some more chum into the water. No sooner said and done than a five-foot shark was suddenly hooked to Weasel's line. We cheered and clapped as the young rascal did battle with the sea-devil. He struggled to gain control of the fish: the veins in his neck were almost bursting through his skin. In fact, he looked like one of those dancers that you just know are about to burn out.

Puffing and panting, whilst desperately trying to remain focused on the job at hand, Weasel struggled on. This shark was one mean motherfucker. Man, it was severely pissed, and who could blame it. The decision was made to cut it loose before it could sabotage the other hook lines – not to mention the whole flippin' boat! The predator quickly swam away before deciding to return and haunt the unlucky fishermen, menacingly circling their boat. What a bummer! I mean, having seen *Jaws* three times, I'd no aching desire to view it again, and starring in a sequel was the last thing on my agenda, especially if my 'parts' were about to start sinking towards the sea-bed.

We were so busy watching the shark, and signalling to one another to sneak the shotgun on to the deck, that we didn't notice the storm heading towards us. Everything seemed to go dark at once; a thunderclap exploded above us and water hammered down. We looked up at the black clouds, and the sea suddenly erupted with activity as a big wave hit the boat. It left us soaked, with Weasel trying to unstrap himself from the chair at the same time as a shark bit into another hook line. Shit! Couldn't we have just settled for a plate of fish 'n' chips?

Touch and I left him to get on with it and ran alongside and into the cabin. Within a few minutes the storm's heart passed directly overhead. Our rushes turned to total fear: could this be life-threatening? It was the sort of experience that made us realise just how powerful Mother Nature really is. Humans strive to control physically everything in their path, but the power of the cosmos is truly something else. For the fifth time in as many years, my life was seemingly in grave danger.

The captain battled against the sea, to get us closer to land and the security of solid rock. Each time we went over a huge wave, the yacht would be hurled upward until it was almost airborne. After which it would come down with a thud, to sink into another swell, which propelled us skyward into the next one. The cabin was a mess. Everything was scattered around the place, so we held firmly on to anything bolted to the ground. You know when someone hits rock bottom, and they think things can't get any worse? Well, apart from having the wrath of the sea to contend with, the boat was still surrounded by sharks and fish eating the chum! Then, suddenly, the boat tilted towards one side: the mast almost touched the water and the crew were just as scared as us. If we could have shit bricks, the boat would have immediately sunk. The nightmare seemed to last for ever, until the storm finally blew over. Just like that – one minute it was there and the next it had moved on . . . like a police patrol or something.

Fucking hell, that was a close one.

We weren't about to take any more chances and ordered the captain to take us back to the girls on the beach. We didn't catch any sharks, but fuck, what a rush!

The Knights of the Round Table were still gripping their seats, eagerly awaiting news of someone being ripped to shreds, but there I had to disappoint them. Instead, a tray of neatly chopped lines was placed on the table and each of us tucked in. Charlie had taken a firm hold on our guests, many of whom were now incapable of talking, but I was on a roll. It was time to relate the story of my fishing trip in Jamaica . . .

You see, it was always the buzz of the hunt, the thrill of the catch and the praise for the capture that appealed to me. My last experience at the mercy of sharks and the ocean had left me slightly wary of being so far out to sea that you can't see land, but at the end of the day, I've always thought that if your time's up, you may as well be doing something that you really enjoy. Don't get me wrong – I could think of a million other ways I'd prefer to go than in the water, but who's choosing?

I was staying in Jamaica with a couple of friends who were building a huge house in a residential area called Ironshore. I made friends with some locals in Montego Bay and was soon on a first-name basis with everyone. They used to call me 'English'. Nice, that.

One night, I was in a bar knocking back Jamaican 100 per cent proof rum. I don't know if any of you have tried this white liquid, but take my word for it, the stuff could run a London Underground train for a whole day. It was so highly flammable that even smoking near a bottle was said to be very dangerous. It put methylated spirits into the Stone Age, and came guaranteed to wipe out any stomach infections – although it might well take your stomach with it. The Yardies guzzle down bottles of this toxic waste, bend up a few women and then take them home for a full session. Lovely. But if I drank more than one glass, the only thing I was good for was a comatose kip!

We were sitting out the back, smoking big spliffs and listening to a Stone Love dance-hall tape. Suddenly a white Jamaican came outside and greeted us with one of the broadest Yardie accents I've ever heard. We touched knuckles and he asked me what I was smoking. I told him to wrap one up.

'Nar, man. Me nar smoke dat,' he said.

'What's wrong with it?' I asked.

'No ting wrong wid it; it just me na smoke dem tinge dare, me just a deal wid the real tinge,' he said.

'Say what, you have it?' I asked, ever the drug-hound.

'Nar, man, but me can get it, if you wan som,' he said, intriguingly. 'Just up sa, bout five minutes' drive; come make we go.'

We drove up into the mountains to an old slavery plantation that was now owned by a Rastaman named Sky. As we approached, a Range Rover with tinted windows came speeding down the driveway. My passenger told me to flash and wave them down. The vehicle pulled up next to us, with reggae music thumping at full blast. The automatic windows slid down, clouds of smoke poured out, and my passenger jumped out and was greeted by two massive Rastafarians. He asked the dreads if they had it, and Sky said to go up to the house and see his mother!

We parked in the forecourt of his huge white house (renamed the Black House – a nice touch, that) and slipped inside. In one of the large rooms there was a group of ten people standing in line waiting to be served. An old woman was sitting on a wooden chair, with a large steel dustbin in front of her. The lid was turned upside-down and was full of weed . . . Hello, Mum!

We joined the queue and waited our turn. Each of the people in front of us asked if she had anything else, to which she replied, 'No.' When it came to our turn, my pal said that Sky had sent us and the woman moved the bin lid. She pulled out some buds the size of my arm. I asked how many she had and how much for all of them.

It was £35 for five – what a bargain! We drove back to the bar and put a bud on the table for everyone to skin up. After one joint of the Alaskan weed, we were all seriously stoned. It was – and is – the strongest puff I've ever smoked, or am ever likely to. I was off it.

Another local Caucasian came out the back and joined our beanie-eyed merry circle. After asking me if it was cool to put a joint together, he proceeded to break a finger-sized bud from the stash. I wasn't taking the piss when I asked him if he was gonna put the whole bud in one joint, but he said it was a small bud and he regularly smoked much bigger ones than the one he was about to roll! We were only on our first joints and everyone in the room showed visible signs of being bombed out. I wasn't concerned at the size of the bud, I just wanted to see how he handled the weed.

Pretending not to focus on the man and his joint, I watched him from the corner of my eye. My suspicions were confirmed when I noticed he'd only crumbled half the bud into the paper. He took about four deep tugs on the joint, then quietly let it go out. After half an hour he got up to leave and asked if he could take the other half of the bud. I reminded him of his earlier statement, made not more than 60 minutes previously, and told him that if he'd smoke it now, I'd give him another bud just as big . . . He left with the spliff that he rolled and walked with a spring in his step to a four-wheel-drive parked outside.

The three brothers who owned the bar were very keen fishermen, and I suppose it was inevitable that they'd invite me out for a spot of Caribbean fishing. At this point I was drunk and red-eyed. Yeah, fishing, great move! We went down to Claude's small boat, and set sail into the night. Each of the Yardies had a machete with them, which is a not uncommon sight: a machete to the Carib is like a Swiss army knife to a camper – an essential tool.

There were six of us in the boat. Saxon played on the blaster and the boys were on the rum, which I steered well clear of. I'd rather get called a weak-heart English boy than pass out in a coma on the deck. It was a totally chilled atmosphere: stars sparkled against a royal blue backdrop and the calm sea reflected the rays of the moon. We got about a mile out before weighing anchor above a multicoloured coral reef, which appeared illuminated by the moon. One of the brothers, Junior, flicked a switch and a set of lights came on, mounted around the vessel's bow. I enquired about the rods or nets and everyone started laughing.

'Nar worry, English, ya safe. We na need net or noting else, broda, just hold on likkle while longer, and the fish will come to us, see,' announced Claude.

We sat around smoking and having a general conversation, listening to the anvil-heavy Studio One tapes. Junior turned the music down and said we were ready.

'Ready for what?' I asked.

He gave me a machete, telling me to be careful with it. The third brother, Whylie, told me to look over the side, where hundreds of fish were swimming around the boat. I'd never seen so many in one place before: they were practically trying to get on to the deck. Apparently the lights attracted fish for miles around, with the hope of being fed by fishermen. It immediately dawned on me that their ancient method of catching fish was to entice them to the boat, then chop the poor buggers up. The lights went out and the fishermen starting bringing their tools down into the water. It was like a war zone – the geezers were going mad and working as fast as they could. I stood in disbelief, as the lads raged war on water-world. After fifteen minutes they stopped; two of them jumped into the water and started throwing the floating corpses on board. In no time at all the boat was filled with pieces of dead fish. Claude started the engine and off we went. The Yardies were falling all over the fish, laughing.

'English, w'happen? Ya all right, broda, sa we do it, ya kna. We na have time fa net and dem bizzinezz; saw we run tinges yere sa,' said Whylie, as I struggled to understand what the fuck he was on about.

'Yeah, man, I'm all right. You guys are fucking crazy,' I spluttered.

'Well, na every won do it like dis,' said Claude. 'When we done ere, we take de fish down town and give way dem to de people dem.'

I left them at the harbour to get on with it; I thought it was barbaric. But, by the same token, things are really hard out there. I went home and crashed out on the veranda while watching the sunrise.

The mass of bodies filling the Havin' It porch area were transfixed by my fishing story before they burst into laughter. I was very bladdered by this point, so I went inside to lie down. A dishevelled DJ, Pants, spun all the latest tracks. For someone who had never taken drugs, his stamina matched that of anyone who did. One of his classic statements was 'I don't need drugs, I'm on a natural buzz', which wasn't entirely true, because he drank shitloads of vodka and Red Bull. Still, we had to hand it to him. In the four months there, the internationally known DJ was always the last person left standing after every session. Not only did he outdo the people using class-As, but he'd play the appropriate music until the villa was either empty or everyone had crashed out.

The end of the party was still a long way off, so Pants – who loved his work – was in his element. Four of the island's biggest promoters were in attendance, which increased the odds of him getting work from them. Three other DJs (Blocko, Peezy and

Owen Clarke), two dancers, eight groupies and nine PRs were also in the house. But, ominously, the entire clan had dropped a trip each and were acting a little crazy. Spurred on by the others, Pete Bones and Daniel were trying their hardest to push the swimming pool closer to the villa and into the shade. But for some reason they didn't succeed, which seemed to really upset them, not to mention the sun worshippers, who patiently waited for the pool to move. Suddenly the boys began chucking girls into the water. I was now sitting at the head of Arthur's table. I spotted Ed and John suspiciously plotting to throw someone in the pool. They walked towards me, so I leapt to my feet and threatened them with a bottle. John was a bit taken aback by my reaction and ran into the villa. I s'pose it was rather alarmist!

Still, I thought nothing more about it until Ed told me that John was very distressed by what had happened, because the LSD had magnified the confrontation by a hundred! I was only fooling, really, but apparently John thought I'd do him, regardless of not getting bunged in. The funny thing was, if they'd really gone for it, I would have let them chuck me in.

Anyway, I felt really bad that John thought I'd do him with a bottle, and I made a solemn promise that – no matter how off it we got – I wouldn't start fighting with my mates, or anyone else. John said he was only gonna ask for a spliff and wouldn't have dreamt of throwing me into the water. Bah, bloody drugs! I broke off a chunk of rocky and handed it to John, who happily accepted my lovely token of real guilt.

As the others searched for Atlantis in the swimming pool, Miranda and Sophie volunteered to cook a fry-up for Captain Nemo and his mermaids. The open-plan kitchen had a big fridge, which came to life when its huge door freeze-framed open. The colours were so bright that Miranda had to close it immediately and grab some shades. Both wearing sunglasses, the girls returned to the fridge. I knew the drugs were taking hold, as Sophie suddenly burst into fits of laughter because the yoghurts had also donned shades and were sprouting legs, arms and mouths! The banana, strawberry and blackcurrant cartons were singing 'La Luna': 'To the beat of the drum . . . Bang! To the beat of the drum. Bang bang!'

She laughed so much that she began coughing violently and choked on her own saliva. Miranda rubbed her back until she calmed down. The fridge, which was still open, had by now returned to normal, so they got the food needed to prepare an elaborate combination of red meat and greasy dairy products. Oddly enough, though, Miranda could soon feel something moving inside the egg she was about to crack open into the frying pan. Placing it in the palm of her hand, she felt the egg wobble from side to side. She looked over at the other eggs, and they too were wobbling like Dibble! The rations of bacon were dragging themselves across the Formica top, while the sausages were rolling up and down beside them. Sophie, in her own world, stared at the running tap, laughing out loud every few seconds.

I ran into the kitchen and found them acting like a right pair of nutters . . . this is *me*, thinking *they* were mad, you understand. Soon enough, though, they came round and decided not to cook after all (thank goodness) and dived in the swimming pool to join the others. Alice was taking underwater pictures of everyone sitting in chairs around a table. Before long, though, the coffee tables, lamps, sunbeds, blankets, pots, pans, clothes and bottles of champagne were also at the bottom of the pool. Barmy!

Bored with splashing about, Ed soon challenged some new arrivals to a vodka-sniffing contest. He convinced them that anyone who came to the villa had to snort alcohol, or they wouldn't be welcome. The girls were let off with a caution, but the lads who came with them had to do it. Ed was something of a connoisseur when it came to snorting vodka: he could do five consecutive spoonfuls without so much as a whimper. If that doesn't sound like much, it's surprising how much damage a tablespoon can do to your head. Snorting is like necking a treble shot, and it stings like fuck.

The lads foolishly followed Ed . . . One of them puked up and the others took their clothes off and jumped into the pool, which prompted Ed to tell them that they'd gone too far and he'd chuck them out for indecent exposure! No one was allowed to run about bollock-naked, unless they were bona-fide friends or females . . . At least, that was what he told the streakers when he kicked them out.

## Spanish Highs

Robbie (Eden), wearing a Burberry skirt and boots, was recovering from delayed reaction caused by a plastic bottle being thrown in the air, which he'd seen coming down as broken 'glass'. At this crucial point, Danny Dred explained that he'd dropped a tab in everyone's drink just over an hour ago: some people minded, but the rest went with the flow. Darkness came in the blink of an eye. It was about ten o'clock when we left the Canin' It villa and drove to the old town.

The enchanting monastery within the walls of the town was lit up against the sky. It was breathtaking, really, an awe-inspiring creation of geometry, craftsmanship and arithmetics. I loved every minute of the buzz and seemed drawn to this historic monument whenever I saw it. Perhaps I was a monk in a previous life. Certainly I've had lots of nasty habits.

There were six of us in the tiny Corsa – all good friends who knew one another's personalities like the backs of our own hands. After finding a convenient parking space, we pushed our way through the crowded streets en route to the Rock Bar in Ibiza Town, which was a well-known playground of the rich and famous. The streets looked more like the catwalks of London, Paris, Milan or New York: everyone was out to party.

There were bars and restaurants on both sides of the narrow walkways. Attractive, radiant PRs would politely ask us if we'd like to drink in their bars. Ann felt more or less normal, until she noticed a luminous object attached to a piece of string, which a man heading towards her was wearing. The brilliant glow stood out more than anything else, and kept her transfixed on the object. By now he'd noticed that she was staring at him, and when we got close enough he stopped and said hello. His whole chest and neck were lit up by the object. He told her it was an adult Buddha from Thailand, and that it wasn't 'glowing' – it was made of wood! She showed so much interest in the Buddha that he eventually handed it to her as a present. Ann wouldn't normally take anything from a stranger, but she took this without hesitation and gave him a huge hug, before rushing to catch up with us.

Danny Dred had been thinking about getting a tattoo, so he asked Sally if she'd accompany him. They went off to the parlour while the rest of us stopped at Derrick's bar for drinks.

The French tattooist, Jean-Pierre, was just finishing a fire-breathing dragon on a Spaniard's back. The geezer was totally pissed up, which obviously helped considerably because he was happily absorbing the pain. Hopefully the LSD would do the same for our man Dred . . . Well, that was the hope!

There was one more person in line before Danny, which allowed him time to consider carefully his indelible stamp. With thousands to choose from, finding a decent symbol that reflected his personality, without going over the top, wasn't going to be easy. I don't suppose they'd have been too keen on drawing a massive line!

He couldn't help but listen to the conversation between the Frenchman and the Moroccan, some guy called Rocky, in front of him. Rocky had decided he wanted an Aboriginal Dreamtime lizard, which represented a spirit of the earth. He told the artist he wasn't very good at dealing with self-inflicted pain but no matter what happened, he had to complete the tattoo. The artist informed him he might feel a rush that would make him dizzy or even pass out, which Rocky took as an insult and warned him not to treat him, a client, like a boy. He'd been to the 'gates of hell' and come back, he insisted, so a tiny needle could do no harm!

He was almost ranting at the tattooist, and Danny and Sally watched on, speechless at what they were hearing.

Rocky sat facing them with his right arm to the artist and told him not to take heed of anything he said. Our pair smiled, although they were feeling slightly intimidated. As soon as the needle touched Rock man's skin, the feller passed out! Danny and Sally couldn't control their laughter, and had to go outside for a few minutes to walk it off. When they went back into the parlour, the artist was bringing Rocky round with smelling salts and making him drink salt water. Rocky felt really embarrassed but told him to continue before he changed his mind. The second the needle touched his arm he was again out like a light bulb. This time, though, he recovered quite quickly and told the artist to carry on and not listen to him. I wonder why!

During the whole painful experience Rocky hurled a number of death threats at the artist, telling him that when the tattoo was complete he was going to pluck his eyes out and squash them on the floor, while his girlfriend watched! He threatened Jean-Pierre's family, said he'd blow the shop up, carve his own tattoo into the artist's face and loads of other equally insane stuff. Sally and Danny didn't say a word the whole time, but just looked on in amazement. It took the best part of three hours, during which Rocky accused the artist of targeting him intentionally, and promised to kill him when it was all over. By the time he did finish, Rocky couldn't have been more apologetic about his behaviour. Sally and Danny looked at one another and ran out of the shop!

The rest of us had already accepted and washed down a number of chapitos. In true Indiana spirit, we moved on. You could tell by the look in John's eyes that he was not of this planet. Paranoid as fuck, he drove us mad with wild allegations of being watched by the police. It was wrong to say things couldn't have got much worse, though, because when you're as high as we were that day, nothing is predictable.

John was walking backwards to look out for any suspicious strangers who might be following us. Ahead of us was a parade of 'goblin'-type people who were promoting Privilege! They had long crooked noses and were covered from head to foot in blue and pink paint. He turned smack, bang, wallop into one of the goblins and suddenly screamed the place down. It took all five of us to restrain him. We were a bit shaky after this episode, so when we got to the Rock Bar, a bottle of tequila was ordered and inevitably washed down in record time. The others were busy trying to work out what colour balls were what on the pool table . . . Me? I felt sick, so I went out for some air. Opposite the bar was the harbour: a set of stairs took you up and along the harbour wall, until you reached the entrance to the port.

It was quite dark, with sea on both sides of the wall, as I sat at the end and faced right out to sea. It seemed that there were voices on the wind. Suddenly, I saw floating gracefully across the waves what looked like a seagull, which turned out to be a swan.

There aren't any swans in Ibiza! I thought.

But, as it drew closer, I saw the white-feathered bird wasn't alone: more and more of them were landing in the sea from the dark sky above. Laughing out loud, I knew it was a hallucination, but all the same I couldn't take my eyes from the swans, although, whilst taken aback by this whole picture, I certainly hoped the birds wouldn't shit on my poor head! No sooner had I allowed this negative thought to enter my head than the birds – in complete synchronisation – took flight. I rose to my feet, hands in the air, and pleaded with the birds to come back.

Locked within a twilight world, I didn't hear the footsteps behind me. Suddenly, a hand on my shoulder caused me to jump with fright, losing my balance, and I hit the rocks before falling into the sea. Managing to cling on to a rock with the tips of my fingers, I found two policemen suddenly leaning down and dragging me back on to solid ground.

'QUÉ PASA, SEÑOR? YOU ARE CRAZY!' one of them shouted in my face.

I tried to muster an intelligible sentence.

'I – am – very – sorry – but please I must go home – before – I – am – sick,' I gurgled, shaking from cold and fear.

'SENOR – YOU – GO – NOW!'

I thanked them, before heading back to the Rock Bar . . . a right wet dreamer!

The journey back to the villa was a really strange one. At one point we were flagged down by another car, which had a famous DJ sparked out on the back seat. Apparently he'd slipped into a trance and didn't know where he was. At sixteen stone, he was quite a handful. He seemed stable enough not to be driven to hospital, so we tried to get him home instead. I knew him very well, so my voice tended to reassure him as he came round, which was probably the first recorded incidence of my chompers having this effect! Although he was grunting and groaning, I loved this man as much as any man could love someone of the same sex without being gay. I also knew that, having gone on enough five-day benders to surmise one another's limits, DJ 'Anonymous' would soon get over the rush and return to his old self again.

He, like the others, had started his marathon that Sunday at Space, where the DJ and I had dropped our first pill at 9.30 in the morning. By the time we'd reached 'Love It' at Pacha that evening, we'd already necked ten Es each and were merrier than a bunch of coal miners at shower time. We went to the after-party for a while, then home to sleep it off. Hours later the torture continued until we caught up with Ed, which was where we now were again.

Anonymous was slumped on the seat, shaking his head as it tilted back and mumbling to himself, with eyes closed. Sam was worried senseless: she'd never seen her recently united boyfriend in such a lamentable state, and kept him talking so he wouldn't pass out. Anonymous was a brilliant garage DJ and a formidable buzzer. At 34, he regarded himself as a true veteran, a notion backed by half the industry. However, past experience had taught me that my friend was no stranger to losing control.

Someone whom you can trust implicitly is worth their weight in uranium. Luckily, I count myself as one such buddy and, no matter how out of their nuts they all get, if a comrade sends out distress signals I have learnt to act. We carried the almost dead-weight from the car into the apartment block and up to the fourth floor, and I made sure everything was all right until I finally left him in the capable hands of Sam and Kathy.

I felt good about this, and was a bit aggrieved to return to the Havin' It villa to find Ed ranting because someone had used all the Rizlas – and the nearest convenience store was on the other side of town. Yeah, let's all get our priorities right.

John suggested using hot knives to incinerate the rocky, and dug up some knives from the kitchen. Ed helped to prepare the instruments and sliced the top off a plastic bottle to be used as an inhaler. The two knives were heated on the stove until they were piping hot and glowing. Then, once happy, Ed put the inhaler in his mouth, gently touched a tiny piece of hashish with one knife and raised it to the bottle. He squeezed the knives together and sucked up the smoke. Hot knives are amazing, because the ball of pure smoke goes straight to your head at jet-propelled speed and is almost as good as a whole joint. Ed replaced the knives and sat down, coughing his guts out. Meanwhile, John coordinated the binge, carefully applying the hot knives for the girls.

Stax had crashed out on the floor hours earlier, and awoke from his pleasant dreams covered in make-up, with shaven eyebrows and plants sticking out of his nose, mouth and underpants! Lovely! He came over and grabbed the knives, stuck a bit of gear on one and tightly pressed them together, but he was so out of it that the knives slipped and instantly burnt into his cheek.

Startled, Ed rushed him into the bathroom, forced him into the shower cubicle and turned the cold water on to his face. The burn had already started to blister, though, and swelled up in the shape of a butter knife. He was in a lot of pain, but other than take him to Casualty, there wasn't that much we could do about it.

Stax was permanently left with a prominent butter-knife scar on his cheek, a rare outward sign of drug damage. I later returned to the villa to find him lying on a sun lounger with frozen lasagne on his face. Everyone else had crashed and, for the first and only time in six weeks, there was complete silence.

I grabbed a bottle of Jack Daniels, but out by the pool I found one of 'Love It's workers behind some shrubbery, bawling her heart out. The narcotics had done for her: Rosa had no idea why she was crying, except to say that she was feeling terribly depressed. She looked awful, with horrible phlegm from her nose running into her mouth. But it wasn't the first time I'd seen someone suffering internal blues: nearly everyone who canes Ecstasy seems to achieve this emotional milestone at some point.

I stayed with Rosa until she was all right, proffering some medicinal Jack Daniels, and finally we fell asleep in one another's arms.

In my dreams, I saw a large white bird, high above me in the sky. It was a swan, and it appeared to be – oh no, it was – it was . . . dropping something!

SPLAT!

That did it. I was never doing drugs again . . .

For a few days, at least.

# **17** On the Run

One night we were all sitting around the table at the Havin' It villa when someone told us a bedtime story . . .

A criminal fellowship of conmen, pickpockets, burglars, armed robbers and thieves met at a service station a few miles from Heathrow airport. To describe them as gangsters would be a misconception – the syndicate viewed themselves merely as entrepreneurs working on the flip-side of the law and economics.

As Bernard crudely put it, 'Without crime there's no fear; without fear there's no control; without control there's no power; without power there's anarchy; and where there's anarchy – me, old son! You'll find people like us always trying to screw the system any way we can. Cos, believe you and me, these bastards need us to divert attention from the real fucking criminals, mate. Gangsters, us? We're fucking school kids by comparison.'

Their petty-crime sprees tended to gross between one and five grand a man, depending on their luck and their time away. It often started at the airport, where any opportunity to steal something was met with open bags. They were experts. By the time they were buckled safely into their seats on the plane, brand-new video cameras, portable CD players and Walkmans would be nestling comfortably with their new, if temporary, owners.

In teams of two, the group set off on pre-planned routes through Europe and arranged to meet a few days later in Ibiza. Bernard and Keith were going via Portugal and, on arriving in Lisbon, the duo immediately went about changing stolen travellers' cheques worth three grand. It worked like a charm.

They had a munch and a drink in town, then the pair decided to search for a hotel to crash out in for the night. Whilst meandering around the city centre, they stumbled across a parked motor crammed with bags and suitcases. On closer inspection, they found the doors unlocked and the keys still in the ignition. Talk about a gift horse! They didn't need a moment to think about it and, with the ease of natural owners, they jumped in and burnt rubber. Driving towards the Portuguese/Spanish border, they stopped to check their haul of passports, credit cards, cash, cameras, jewellery and designer clothes. Lovely!

They'd mastered their 'profession' whilst travelling abroad to football games. As well as becoming hardened hooligans, they'd earnt a pound note or two and used the match crowds as cover – the logic being that there were so many English people in the cities that finding detached bands of thieves presented even more unwanted hard work for the police forces and Interpol. If the law did ever catch up with them, the situation could erupt into a full-scale battle between the English visitors, home-team fans, the Old Bill and riot squads.

Make no mistake, these boys were handy. If the law came on top of them while they were stealing, they'd either run with it anyway or put it down, apologise and walk calmly from the premises. To attempt to stop them would have invited Gawd-knows-what: these lads had all been to prison many times and weren't inclined to pay a return visit.

Their exploits in Europe brought them into contact with buyers from countries all over the continent, which meant that by the time they reached the borders, cash and stolen documents would be the only illegal items in their possession. Their Euro counterparts were only a phone call away and usually purchased everything available: whether or not the goods came from a fellow-countryman was never something to question. The buyers always came with hard currency, although never really enough. The thieves were the first to admit they felt slightly conned each time a trade took place, but that was the nature of things. It wasn't as if they'd had to pay anything for the stuff in the first place!

After meeting their Portuguese connection, it was en route to the border for Bernard and Keith, where dressing smartly generally meant a smoother passage through customs into safer territory. Once there, they hired another car using a stolen licence and credit card. They were pleased with their quick haul, not to mention the fact that their pockets were bulging, which made the drive that bit less gruelling. As they stopped in small towns on the way, a further £1,800 was changed from cheques found in the car. They left the vehicle at Barcelona airport, where they booked flights to Ibiza for later on that night.

By the time Bernard and Keith arrived at the villa, the rest of the team was already there. It was a beautiful day, and the swimming-pool area resembled a laid-back London fashion house, with gorgeous women lazing everywhere. Roy Ayres played loud on the stereo, as the lads gathered around different tables talking shop. An electrical Aladdin's Cave lit up the villa's pristine interior. It seemed that the ten-man crime spree has caused quite an eruption in Europe and had sparked off a plague of false insurance claims.

John went on to explain that the villa had been double-booked, so they could only stay there for another day. A plan was concocted whereby everyone would travel together to Marbella, which annoyed Bernard and Keith, who'd only just got there and hadn't even had chance to see Ibiza Town. They decided to go instead to a holiday complex they'd seen on the way to the villa, and book an apartment there for five days. Things seemed sweet.

The following morning Keith went into the old town whilst Bernard slept like a baby. On almost every corner was a designer retail store, selling various items at exorbitant prices. As he walked by a jewellery shop, Keith's keen fox-like senses sprang into life and he nipped into the store. Twiddling his thumbs and humming while a Gypsy Kings track played on the radio, he waited for five minutes, before an assistant came out front to serve him.

'I'm looking for a diamond engagement ring, mate,' he insisted. He spent over 20 minutes examining a wide selection of rings and their prices. He bartered relentlessly with the woman on the price of a diamond, until she agreed to let him have it for just under two grand, whereupon he cheerfully left the store promising to return with his brother-in-law and the money.

Keith rushed up to the complex for reinforcements. Sports bag in hand, the partners went back to the store a couple of hours later. They slipped through the door without making a sound, and were soon pocketing entire trays of rings, necklaces, watches and earrings. Keith replaced each tray from whence it came, then leant over the unmanned counter to open a cabinet full of diamond rings. He grasped three trays and wrenched them from the display unit, causing the glass door to slam, making a loud, smashing sound.

'Quick, let's move,' announced Bernard, as they high-tailed it out the door.

Immediately the assistant appeared and tried to grab Keith, but was pushed to the ground as the convicts made their escape. Separating, they ran through the narrow streets, dodging the sound of police sirens on their separate routes to the apartment. Keith reached the safe-house first, but Bernard didn't show until over an hour later. They peered through the closed blinds, spotting a group of Spaniards dressed in shirts and ties, wandering the complex. Keith thought they were Dibble and tried to convince Bernard to go back to the other villa before it was too late. Bernard insisted that his mate was over-reacting, but Keith didn't want to risk being captured and decided to chance reaching the villa without detection.

Keith is a big lump, a real potato, but somehow he'd convinced Bernard they should drop their haul at the house in a rucksack, and off he went. He got to the villa and stashed the gems before greeting his mates, who were almost ready to leave. Most of their stuff had already been packed and sent ahead in another vehicle. Three hours passed slowly, and it dawned on him that Bernie must have been nicked. Clean out of ideas, Keith went back to the apartment. Walking through the grounds, he noticed the same group of Spaniards in the complex manager's office. When they saw the fugitive, the hit-squad rushed towards him. But if there was one thing in Keith's favour, it was his fitness. He left them standing.

As soon as the Spaniards were out of sight, he ran into an

apartment block, climbing the steep staircase and using a bit of acrobatics to get onto the roof. He lay there in hiding for hours, hoping not to be discovered. As soon as the coast seemed clear, he came down out of the block . . . and walked straight into a waiting trap.

'Oh SHIT!'

Over fifteen officers pounced on him, grabbing hold of every limb. Taken to the police station, he was soon reunited with Bernard, who it turned out had been arrested by the same hit squad, soon after Keith had left the apartment. The shop assistant was brought in to identify the perpetrators. The officers told them that if the stolen property was returned straight away, they would be deported and not sent to prison. Keith didn't trust them, but Bernard said they had no option but to give the stuff back. An armed guard escorted them to the villa. Thinking and hoping their friends had already left, Keith and Bernard plus the Spanish Armada drove into the grounds of the luxury pad.

The rest of the firm were in their motors and just about to leave when the happy group got there. Keith showed the officers where he'd hidden the treasure trove and promised sincerely that his friends knew nothing about it. Which they didn't, so he wasn't telling porkies. However, Dibble arrested everybody they thought connected with the robbery. This enraged the group, because the boys had broken an important golden rule: 'Thou shalt not bring Old Bill back to a villa housing wanted criminals and an assortment of stolen property!'

Luckily, the goods were probably cruising the Spanish open road by now, and the lads had nothing illegal that warranted a nicking, especially after Keith and Bernard were caught bang to rights. Hours later, the group was set free, barring Bernard and Keith, who were charged with armed robbery (apparently Keith had had a weapon). The brothers-in-arms were taken directly to court, where a judge ordered their detention pending further investigations. Going to prison in England was one thing – but to be banged up in a Spanish nick was another altogether. Put it this way, they're not flippin' holiday camps!

Luckily the duo were being transported to the same prison, so they weren't really too bothered. The Mexican-style clink had four watchtowers, one on each corner of the massive concrete walls surrounding the perimeter boundaries. The sharp-eyed, armed guardsmen were under strict orders to fire one warning shot at anyone attempting to escape, and a second to take their lights out. Neither Keith nor Bernard fancied that. The antiquated prison was divided into categories of Under-21s, Over-21s and a women's section, which was further split into related groups. As they were led in, prisoners on both sides of the landing laughed and screamed at them in Spanish.

After being washed down with a hosepipe and receiving their allocation of itchy bed linen, Bernard was admitted to the Over-21s wing, whilst Keith was escorted up to the Under-21s on the second landing, where most of the earlier laughter had come from. The youngsters in the section were still out to prove a point. Like impressionable people the world over, the inmates in this section felt they had something to prove and would often respond to situations they couldn't handle verbally with brute force. Inmates inside such institutions were always prone to violent behaviour: they had no choice. Nobody gave a fuck, so they had to show others they didn't take no shit. It was a volatile atmosphere of paranoia and loathing, ready to erupt at any moment.

Keith wasn't feeling very confident: some of the prisoners were just as big as he was, and he might be in danger, for all he knew. The guard signalled to his *amigo* and the electronic, steel cell doors slid open. The grubby cell was tiny, with a five-foot bed in the corner and a broken plastic window with bars outside.

They'd arrived in time for dinner, so they were ushered down to the dining hall, where 200 young offenders had to wait for their name to be called before they could get their food. Keith couldn't speak a word of Spanish and didn't even recognise his name being yelled loudly in Spanish, until the guard slapped him round the head, which of course caused a flurry of laughter around the hall.

The fish and leftover soup reeked of the River Thames. There was no way he was gonna to eat that crap. All the prisoners were allowed a bottle of beer with their dinner, so Keith quickly necked the cold San Miguel. He noticed that none of the others were drinking their beers, but instead were discreetly passing the bottles along, until they reached a table where the wing's so-called 'Daddy' sat. That was a simple conclusion. Why else would anyone forfeit their beverage, when it was the only alcohol-based refreshment they could have?

The Daddy was slightly bigger than Keith, who couldn't fathom why the others were so afraid of him. If it came to the crunch, Keith would be more than willing to go all the way with this guy. Being a new foreign face, it was only a matter of time before someone would try and test him, but Keith was quite ready to kick arse and show them he wasn't fucking about.

Later that evening, in the exercise yard, Big Daddy waved for Keith's attention, but got no response. A group of five approached him and pointed to the toilets. Keith couldn't work out what they were saying and walked away from them. As he did this, Big Daddy motioned for Keith to follow them into the toilet. Warily, he did so. The Daddy then pointed at his trainers and sweatshirt, as if he wanted Keith to take his clothes off. Keith refused and, squaring up to the big man, punched him square on the nose. Immediately the others attacked him with small coshes and knocked him to the ground. Alarm bells rang out throughout the prison. Wielding batons, a horde of screws charged the bogs, where the other convicts were standing in a straight line against the wall. Just as he'd learnt to do in his hooligan days, Keith was curled up in a ball on the floor. He was dragged back to the cells and locked in for the night. Some welcome!

Breakfast was just as tense while he was sitting amongst the predominantly Spanish inmates. Back in the exercise yard, the mood was hotting up. Big Daddy was flanked by a posse, and again pointed at the toilets, beckoning Keith to follow them. With no knowledge of how long they planned to keep this up, he decided to make a stand, but trailed happily behind the group. The toilets were the only place that weren't monitored by the guards or CCTV. Once in the lavs, the others stopped and surrounded Keith, who reacted by headbutting the Daddy, knocking him unconscious. The others nervously took a step back, so Keith barged through them and out into the yard.

Following that incident his remaining four months were considerably easier, because no one would dare even to look at him. He didn't see Bernard for the whole time he was there. Sometimes they communicated through their Spanish lawyers, who were appointed for them by concerned parents back in London. The lawyers got them released on conditional bail, the terms being that they paid 310,000 pesetas bail-money in advance, and they were restricted to Ibiza and prohibited from travelling by boat or plane. After leaving the court room, the lads went to a designated hotel, where they met up with some Spanish friends, who brought them fake identities and passports. Hours later they touched down on British turf, enjoying their newly found freedom.

# **18** Sex Crimes

Thousands of people flock to Ibiza each year in the hope of finding some work for the summer season. The arduous positions available are usually the mundane kind of jobs that no Spaniard would do – certainly not for the money being offered – and so are tailor-made for English Johnny Tourists wishing to fund their partying. Equally, vacancies are offered to English people because the job description (which is often rewritten daily) involves dealing with English-speaking customers. The conditions are crap, though. Wages can sometimes amount to a measly few pounds, whilst the working day seems to get longer and longer, and then longer again.

Ibiza has thousands of bars and restaurants, all in need of staff. Most positions are filled by the beginning of the season. Young international travellers from all walks of life are drawn to Ibiza by the perceived – and artificially perpetuated – images of glamorous positions within clubs and catering. Half the time the best jobs have already long gone to friends of the management, or someone with a respected CV.

That hurdle crossed, the hapless employee is catapulted into a daily routine of very hard and very physical work. Being paid next to nothing means that they cannot afford their own apartment and have to mush it with anything up to six other people. Still, it's character building and can serve as a valuable exercise in working and surviving in a foreign state. Some people can handle it, whilst others don't have the stomach for it and return home or, failing that, turn to crime as a way of staying the entire season.

Arriving on the island late, though, doesn't necessarily mean there is no work. Good, reliable staff are hard enough to find under normal circumstances, and being surrounded by some of the best clubs in the world doesn't help matters at all. A lot of the time employees start off with good intentions, but are gradually drawn into the labyrinthine underworld of 24-hour clubbing, and that can mean a spiralling descent.

Lisa was a professional dancer who'd acquired her wonderful talent back in the late eighties, when she'd unveiled her dazzling moves at all the big dance parties. Since then, she'd travelled around South America for a few years, before returning to England. Back in Blighty, she was offered work as a dancer for a London-based entertainment company that was promoting in Ibiza. Having lived and survived in some of the roughest parts of Brazil, she considered herself very streetwise, although people who knew her thought her naïve. She was certainly brassy. Her dress sense left nothing to the imagination, and her inhibitions would take a definite back seat whenever she spotted a *Baywatch* lookalike on the beach, in a club, in the bog and quite possibly up a tree. Anywhere the emotion and the hormones would take her.

Lisa had the kind of front that Marks and Sparks would be proud of, but most girls took an instant dislike to her, especially when their boyfriends were gagging around her, which was often. As soon as Lisa saw someone she fancied, she was off, locking on to the eligible subject like an Exocet missile: WHAM! Long legs, busty cleavage, perky lips and the cheeky grin of a St Trinian sixth-former – she was unstoppable, insatiable. Even walking down the street with her could constitute a dangerous condition. Intoxicated groups of fellas would take turns at blatantly trying to pull her in front of any man, woman or child. It could have been her husband holding her hand, with a rose stuck in his teeth, and they still wouldn't give a toss.

On the other hand, Lisa didn't exactly need back-up. A karate student from an early age, as well as a health and fitness fanatic, she was used to physical contact. If you said she was a beautiful woman, she might well decide to hold it against you. A string of four-letter words was designed to phase any unwelcome would-be suitor; if not, then a swift left foot to the chin would finish matters. Yeah, you got it. Just when you thought it was safe to grab a girl's arse, the sisterhood has gone and learnt karate! Bummer, eh?!

## Spanish Highs

Lisa had arrived in Ibiza six weeks earlier, with her long-term boyfriend Jeff. Jeff was pissed off at the way she'd been conducting herself and, since landing, the usually inseparable happy couple had done nothing but rant and rave about all sorts of bullshit. Lisa encouraged his hot-tempered flare-ups by disappearing for two or more days every time they argued. Although she crashed with friends on most occasions, there had been a few nights when he just wasn't sure – and, to be fair to Jeff, nor were any of her mates. The last time they'd fallen out, Mad Lisa had ended up completely off her nut at a house party, with a couple of well-known womanisers.

As the Roxy Music lyric has it, 'You say "coke", I say "Yes", dim the lights, you can guess the rest' . . . although you might be far, far wrong.

The funny thing was, Lisa did in fact really love Jeff and wouldn't dream of sleeping with anyone else, however silvery their tongues or tempting their invitations. His objections, though, were met with hostility, resentment and accusations of jealousy, which weren't entirely unreasonable. He'd given her an ultimatum: she either flew back to England with him or stayed alone in Ibiza, which was, let's face it, the act of a desperate man. No surprise, then, that Jeff ended up listening to the raindrops falling on to the roof of his flat in Hampstead, whilst Lisa carried on playing in the sunshine. I suppose – put in the same disempowering position – a lot of men would've done exactly what Jeff did, and also maybe knocked a few bods out on the way. Still, that didn't make him feel any better. He knew he'd fucked it up.

Lisa was sitting at a bar on the terrace, after a gruelling shift on the platforms at Amnesia. A couple of northern lads, Bill and Ben, queued up to buy her drinks and give her sniffs of quiver. By 6 a.m., the three of them were blasted, and began the inevitable journey in a taxi back to the boys' gaff to snort more powder. It wasn't such a big deal for Lisa. She'd seen the boys before and loads of people seemed to know them. She thought she was safe. Bad move.

When Lisa was not looking, one of the lads poured her a drink, which he spiked with the fluid of three Temazepams. Narcosis was almost instantaneous. She remembered Bill asking if she minded him taking a photograph of her, but after that everything was hazy. She was actually awoken by some friends who'd found her wrapped in a sarong on the beach. Bruised from head to toe, Lisa had no idea what had happened. Her body felt as it normally did after a steamy session with Jeff. But this was different, very different.

Thinking the worst and not wanting to face anyone, the poor girl shacked up with some female friends for a few days before flying home to Jeff. Her friends knew exactly who the assailants were and decided to tell someone, who they thought could physically do something about it. It turned out that Bill and Ben were well known as a pair of gangsters, who always carried knives. No one wanted to risk being stabbed, because that's how serious it could get; on the other hand, no one wanted them to get away with it, either.

Meanwhile Bill and Ben had confided in Paul and shown him explicit pictures, which depicted Lisa in a fully revealing series of poses with a number of different sex props. Paul knew little about Lisa, but what he did know was that she seemed a decent girl. Something about this cosy little set-up didn't seem right – in fact, it seemed very, very dodgy. His suspicions worsened when the Flowerpot Men went on to tell him how many drugs they'd pumped into her system. Paul didn't like this at all. In fact he wished they hadn't told him – surely this was classified as rape?

Paul's stomach rotted as he silently listened to what they had to say in all its incriminating glory. In the whole summer he'd been in Ibiza, Paul had never heard anything like this. A couple of days later he caught up with some of Lisa's friends, who told him they thought something bad must have happened to her when she refused to discuss it with anyone but her boyfriend, back in London. But Bill and Ben's confession bugged Paul, and it was only a matter of time before he himself confided in his girlfriend, Jan, who was even more angry than Paul. It seemed that a train of events had been set in motion, which could only have one possible conclusion.

As Paul knew full well, Bill and Ben didn't fuck about when it came to violence. He couldn't stand against them alone, even if he was brave enough to take on the task: he'd definitely get a hiding.

Paul and Jan were chilling out in the bedroom of the villa that their friend Shaun had let them use for the summer. Suddenly Bill and Ben and two other big lumps strolled into the bedroom, asking Paul where the pictures were. The gist of the discussion was that the revealing snaps had gone walkabout, and the Flowerpot Men had started to panic. If the photos got into unsympathetic hands, the lads might have criminal charges brought against them – certainly enough to throw away the key for a good while.

Although Paul didn't really like Bill and Ben, the three of them had been out together on many an occasion and he couldn't help feeling that the disrespect they showed him and Jan now was totally uncalled for. But if he said anything out of line, his head would be pounded in.

'If anyone finds out about those photos, the pair of you are battered,' said Bill.

Paul tried reasoning with the Flowerpot Men but, as soon as he did, he was interrupted by one of the other blokes who had come with them.

'Listen 'ere, you, I'll personally cut you ear to fucking ear, if I have to come back.'

Lovely.

The toerags left the couple shaking with fear, wondering if leaving the island was the best option. The two lads were big-time cokeheads – which meant they were paranoid and unpredictable. Days later the telephone rang.

'Oi oi, Paul, you all right, son?'

It was Shaun, who was currently displaying his finest telephone manner. 'I'm at the airport,' he continued. 'I'll be there in about 20 minutes.'

Shaun owned the villa; in fact, Shaun owned quite a lot of things. People who didn't know him would say he's a gangster, but he wasn't really: he just knocked about with villains, because they were the blokes he grew up with. Shaun did share several of their (ahem) principles and morals but, critically, lacked the characteristics that could turn a normal person into a gangster. He was good to have around, though. Just having Shaun on the island made Paul feel more confident and ready for anything.

When he told Shaun what had occurred, Shaun hit the roof. It wasn't just that Bill and Ben had invaded the privacy of his home and threatened its occupants: he was outraged at what had happened to Lisa.

'Where are they now?' Shaun demanded.

The smart money was on Bill and Ben being at the Café del Mar.

Shaun unlocked a wooden box, neatly hidden in the custom-made wardrobe, taking out two baseball bats, two caps (to disguise their appearance) and, for good measure, a tasty Samurai sword. The sword would be useful to ward off any other drinkers who might fancy getting involved.

The three of them sat at a table outside a restaurant next to the café, as Paul pointed Bill and Ben out.

'Paul, go home and wait for us there.'

But Paul was having none of it. Quietly he wrapped a pillowcase around his face and took the sword from Shaun. The lads left the restaurant and parked their motor directly behind the café. A darkened alleyway led them practically straight to where the Flowerpot Men and their cronies were standing. Within minutes all four of them were on the floor, trying to break the heavy blows of the Louisville Sluggers, whilst the nasty sword kept everyone else at bay. Shortly afterwards, the tasty trio made their escape, but not before they'd left their victims with broken bones, cuts and bruises, and severely threatened sex lives.

After making a few phone calls to England, they arranged to borrow a friend's yacht and crew for a while. Hours later the yacht cruised out to Formentera, where the whole group explored the islands for just over a week. On returning, Paul found out that the Flowerpot Men had left the island: partly because the photos had mysteriously disappeared, but at least equally because they'd been given a damned good hiding. No one ever suspected foul play on Paul's part and they all lived happily ever. This wasn't the law of the jungle. It was just – sometimes, if not always – the law of Ibiza.

Party on!

# **19** Aliens in Ibiza!

A lot of Ibiza's fashionable clientele spend their recovery periods on certain beaches around the island. Sa Trincha, a small stretch of sand at the far end of Salinas beach, is one such meeting place. Unlike the commercial sea fronts, Sa Trincha's 'anything goes' policy with regards to nudity and inhibitions captivates all sorts of colourful, chilled and open-minded characters. The open-plan restaurant serves a number of Spanish and European delicacies, while the DJ plays an assortment of ambient, trip-hop and dub plates from early morning to late night. Although the beach has an international flavour, apart from a few British promoters and Ibiza veterans, English people usually stay at the more mainstream Jockey Bar at the other end of the beach. There, DJs play banging house music to over a thousand sun worshippers. The 300 or so people on Sa Trincha are much more laid back, reserving their essential energy for another big night ahead.

So it was in '95. I was feeling nauseous after necking two pills and eating *calamarie*. The beach restaurant served up a top munch at the worst of times and was generally packed solid from dawn until dusk. I adored the batter-shrouded squid rings, even though I usually couldn't stand fish products. But this wasn't about food, it was about getting over the night before at 'Up Yer Ronson'. The adjoining rocks provided a perfect shelter in which to hide away and bring my guts out. The sound and movement of water gently hitting the rocks reinforced the rush, but it was the sickly feeling I couldn't handle.

Silently, I watched a man and woman engrossed in t'ai chi. For over an hour they stretched and moved like ballerinas. Soon enough, they noticed me sitting alone and motioned for me to join them. Yeah, me! The only Thai anything I could handle came on a silver tray with loads of sweet-and-sour. Inevitably I declined but, after introducing themselves, the woman (Ayliesha) pulled a bong from her bag and commenced preparing the home-made device with some really strong-smelling skunk. Ayliesha had been born in Egypt and brought up in England, whilst Hassan was a Mexican brought up in Iraq, Ethiopia and Europe. I gathered that their parents worked for some government operation, but I found the couple fascinating. They spoke spiritually about the earth and solar systems. Both of them knew a lot about astronomy, which is something I'd always wanted to learn about . . . plus, of course, they had this massive bag of weed!

They'd met thirty years ago near Ayers Rock in Australia, where they were both on the run from their governments. I wanted to ask why, but I thought it was too personal. In the end curiosity got the better of me and I just came right out with it.

'Let's just say we didn't agree with our parents' views on world politics,' explained Hassan, intriguingly.

'Do your parents work together?' I enquired.

'Oh, no. They represent the same theology but from different perspectives. Each carrying out their own duties in the name, and for the supposed good, of mankind,' said Ayliesha, obviously unconvinced about that one.

'So . . . ' I continued. 'You've come to Ibiza for the nightlife?'

'No such luck, I'm afraid. We're working on a really important project at the moment, so we don't get much time for clubbing,' she replied.

'If you don't mind me asking, what is it that you do for a living?'

At the time, asking this question felt a bit like asking James Bond where he got his fountain pens.

'No, it's cool,' Hassan insisted. 'I used to be a biochemist and Ayliesha was a marine biologist. But at present we're working with a number of environmental activist groups,' he said.

'Hassan is a wizard computer hacker,' Ayliesha butted in.

Hassan himself expanded.

'I jack into various networks, searching for any hints of

conspiracies against the human race. Once I've found these folders, I leave my own calling card, which is a virus named 'Green fights back'. It deletes their files after I've safely copied them, and leaves a green screen with a picture of an old lady sticking two fingers up! Then I immediately download the data on to the worldwide web, where anyone can read, copy or act on the information they've received.'

This sounded fascinating. Hassan went on to list the kinds of conspiracies he found: mind-control experiments on unsuspecting members of the public; the true meaning of the New World Order; double dealings and secret-service stuff; man-made killer viruses . . . .

'You name it, my friend, and we have found it,' he concluded.

Suddenly Ayliesha asked about my thoughts on Aids.

What did she mean, 'thoughts'?

'Have you ever wondered where it came from or why the medical associations around the world can't find a cure?' she asked. 'Don't you find it a little strange that our scientists can invent satellites that can read the print on a newspaper from thousands of miles away, but can't find a cure for Aids or cancer?'

Since she put it like that, I suppose it did seem rather odd.

'If I was to tell you that Aids is a man-made virus that was created to reduce the world's population, you'd think I was crazy, right?'

I wasn't really sure what to think. Is that what they thought?

'We've said too much,' stated Hassan. 'You enjoy the Ecstasy, my friend. We won't drive you insane with our wild, unseemly accusations.'

But I wasn't going to let them stop there. They had to tell me more.

'OK. Look, first let me tell you how I met Ayliesha,' said Hassan. 'My father is a scientist who works for a top-secret government organisation. Although my mother and I knew the work he carried out was of the utmost importance, we'd never actually ask what he was doing.'

Hassan explained that his father had his own laboratory built into a separate wing of the large house. Security was always very tight: the laboratory was impregnable, and no one else even went to that side of the building. His father would work non-stop for days at a time.

'One morning after one of his three-day sessions, he rushed out of the house leaving one of the lab's windows open,' continued Hassan. 'I went in and was shocked to discover that my father was working on a top-secret time-travel project.'

Whuh? Time travel?!

'Yes, travelling from one space in time, as we know it, to another controlled space in a different time. But let me tell you the story first, then you can ask me questions later. OK?'

OK.

'The date was 1965, and drawings of an aeroplane on a blackboard, with a series of mathematical equations around it, disappeared and reappeared on another blackboard headed "1941". I didn't think much about it until days later, when I read an article in the newspapers about an aeroplane that had completely disappeared in broad daylight as it was coming in to land at Denver airport. This was just two days after seeing the same date on the blackboard. The plane vanished from the radar and was never seen again; nor were its hundreds of passengers.

'The very next day my father received a stack of letters and parcels from the government's confidential postal service. Although he is very security-conscious, he'd sometimes override the security locking process so that he could move freely throughout the wing without punching different lock-codes. On one such occasion I seized the opportunity to find out more about my father's work and found letters speaking of an intergalactic meeting between a specially appointed body, representing the earth, and an alien life-form called The Nefilim.'

Now hang on, this was all getting a bit far-fetched. The Nefilim? Weren't they some sort of Goth band?

Hassan explained that in fact the Nefilim represented a planet called Marduk. Phew, thank God for that! The thought of Fields of the Nephilim with all that flour all over them and horrible pop tunes was far more terrifying than any scene in *Alien 3*.

'It's OK, my friend. I realise this information is hard to grasp,' said Hassan, noticing my scepticism, 'and if I were you, I'd probably be thinking the same thing. But this story is real . . . We can speak about something else if you like.'

We could, but I didn't want to. Of course I was sceptical, and kept expecting Jeremy Beadle. But there was something about this story that captivated me. There was no real reason for him to make the whole lot up.

'It's hard to explain how I felt when absorbing this information,' added Hassan. 'Although happy and excited at the notion of twentieth-century man finally communicating with beings of another galaxy, amongst the top-secret documents I discovered were plans of various experiments using biochemical viruses, designed to kill the aliens so that scientists could carry out detailed autopsies. Their motives were based on that primitive paranoia about being invaded by a stronger stellar force. They spoke of exploiting the aliens' weaknesses and finding a way of killing them before they "destroyed" the planet earth. It was all patriotic propaganda bullshit, really. They also had plans to strip their spacecraft of technology in pursuit of the ultimate weapon.'

This didn't make sense. If the aliens did have the ultimate weapon, how would anyone be able to get anywhere near the spacecraft?

I was quietly pleased with my inscrutable logic.

'A line of communication was established, which is why the ships weren't gonna just burst out of the sky for all to see. This was a top-secret meeting, for authorised eyes only. The aliens had agreed to teach the earth's military scientists intergalactic space- and time-travel, in exchange for precious metals such as gold or platinum.'

Hmmmm . . .

'Anyway, the dark undertones of this meeting with extra-terrestrials suggested that the real men of power wanted the Nefilim dead. I was horrified and very frightened by this news,' insisted Hassan. 'My emotions were thrown into total chaos, as a deep-rooted resentment towards my father flooded me. I filled a box with all the documents I could find and then packed a few belongings. Some friends from university had their own website, so I went straight round to their place and downloaded all the information on to the Internet.

'The place of contact with the aliens was near Ayers Rock in Australia. I used a fake ID to get a new passport and flew to Thailand, where I stayed until two days before the meet. More than anything in my life, I knew that I had to be there and see the aliens for myself.'

As Hassan told it, after arriving in Perth he'd hired a vehicle and driven towards Ayers Rock. It was still a good two days' drive from the airport, so he didn't waste any time stopping on the way, until he came across Ayliesha, who was hitch-hiking to the Rock in the hope of 'witnessing aliens landing on earth'.

'I asked where she'd heard this and she said, "On the Internet," ' he rambled. 'When I told her it was me who downloaded the secret files, it was as if fate had brought us together. You'd think it ended there, but we picked up a convoy of at least 30 cars en route to the Rock for the same reason. I actually thought we would save the world: but considering we didn't have so much as a Swiss army knife between us, I wasn't sure how on earth we were going to do it.

'We finally reached the area described in the files, roughly two hours before showtime. There were no signs of life for miles around, and if anyone was watching us, the full beam of our headlights was a dead giveaway.'

He gazed across Ibiza, pausing before continuing the story.

'Ayliesha spotted the faint flicker of a light,' Hassan related, 'off the road across the dark plains. We all got out of our vehicles, making our way on foot in the general direction of the dimming light. Suddenly, without warning, a high-pitched sound rang out from all around us and everything went blank.'

What happened then?

'When we opened our eyes,' he said, 'we were hundreds of miles from where we originally got out of the vehicle. But what really freaked us out was the fact that we were alone. All the other cars had disappeared, as if they weren't there in the first place. Neither of us knew how we got there or where we were. The time was 6.25 a.m. – we'd somehow lost four and a half hours!

'We must have been on to them, because we were knocked

out by some sort of man-made electrical sonic boom,' the t'ai chi man added. 'We left Australia the same day and have been travelling the world ever since. I wouldn't say we were freedom fighters, but we do try our best to expose things! You won't believe the shit that's happening in the world today.'

They were right there. I didn't believe this story at all, and asked who sent them to wind me up so ridiculously.

'You believe what you want to, my friend,' concluded Hassan. 'I think I've said enough already, and it's getting quite late. There's only one way to beat the evils of society and that, Wayne, is through a higher consciousness, purpose and understanding. We must go now. Be happy and true to yourself, and I hope we will meet again one day. By the way, who's Beadle?'

That was it. They'd convinced me: they were having a larf, taking hideous advantage of my fragile, addled state, and the fact that I was the biggest E'd-up sausage-making machine that ever walked the earth.

Several days later I read about a large number of people having seen a large, unidentifiable light over Ibiza. Some people even claimed to have pictures of the UFO. Is everything ready on the dark side of the moon?

Lights, cameras and cue the music!

# **20** Hidden Agenda

Our romance grew in strength with the dawn of each summer's day. Sally was a beautiful budding musician, studying global politics at university in northern England. Until that point in her life, she'd never planned on becoming a politician – far from it. She'd wanted to help like-minded people by introducing them to the real world.

Sally had witnessed the three Summers of Love in 1987, '88 and '89, and didn't regret her drug-consuming exploits for one minute. She felt that those early years, when Ecstasy had just been discovered, were very different from today. The drug had enhanced her life, opened up her positive thinking and the emotion we term 'love'. That was why she took the pill: when people dropped E, it brought out a whole new person, who felt no discrimination against anyone or any living thing. But once she could access that world of unity and brighter horizons without pharmaceuticals, she didn't waste any time in declaring that enough was enough. Since then, she hadn't even contemplated taking any kind of mind-altering substance, including alcohol.

In the old days she, like millions of young people, had no regard for politics or the workings of the world. She didn't blame anyone for dropping out of the rat-race in search of the next high. It was so very easy for most people to get sucked into the dreaded cycles and entrapment of modern-day society. In many ways, her own politicisation had come about through Ecstasy.

'If we let them take away our right to vote as citizens,' she'd say, 'we might as well give up completely.'

Perhaps slightly naïvely, Sally felt that traditional

parliamentary democracy was the way the younger generations could influence the future of the planet, taking it away from the segregated, demoralised, closed-minded, half-baked, double-dealing warmongers of those currently in power.

Still, Sally never pulled any punches when expressing her opinions, which is why we got on. I'd been a bit of a lad in the past myself, but was now discovering the security of knowledge and self-development.

At fifteen, I'd been expelled from school with an acute form of dyslexia, after spending a few years hijacking trucks containing household goods, and thieving anything not bolted down. Then came the parties and the promoting. By the time I met Sally, though, I was content to earn a small weekly wage as a consultant for a record company that specialised in releasing music geared for the dance industry. Like Sally, it wasn't until after the Summers of Love that I realised just how misinformed I was.

By the age of 29, I was learning all the time and taking in as much as I could. My whole personality and attitude to life were totally different from what they had been only two years previously. I was always reading, often feeling like a giant sponge soaking up information and deciphering it into my own way of thinking. Some people called me 'deep'; I preferred to think I was just spiritually awakened.

Sally and I rarely argued, although we tended to differ when it came to who really ran the country. My view was – and is – that all the political parties are excessively dictated to by corporate industrialists, and always would be. But apart from this subject causing a rift or two between us, the relationship was generally as blissful as it got. Then again, we'd only been together for three weeks, so there was plenty of time for potatoes.

Sally had booked a holiday in Ibiza with two girlfriends, who wanted a break from studying. She invited me along and booked a flight on the Wednesday, with us all leaving on the Friday. None of the others had been to Ibiza before and they were really looking forward to chilling out on the beaches by day, eating in good restaurants by night. No hassle, no stress, no drugs, no clubs and no getting drunk. Nothing but total relaxation, sun worshipping and, well, frenetic sexual activity!

We were met at the airport by Sally's brother, Glen, and his drop-dead gorgeous girlfriend Heika, from Germany. They'd been dossing around Europe for six months before agreeing to stay in Ibiza for a while. Their home for the next two weeks would be an authentic Spanish villa located in Es Canar, in the east of the oft-titled 'magical island'.

At first light on our first full day Glen took us on a quick tour of the isle, ending later that night at a bar in the old town. Unbeknown to me, Glen was bisexual, which is why we were drinking in a predominantly gay bar. Standing in a gay bar is not really my idea of a good time, but if I grin and bear it, I can just about get by.

The following days were spent on various beaches within close range of the villa and out of the reach of tourists. By the fourth night, though, I made excuses and Sal and I started doing our own thing. We were both connoisseurs of good food and soon found three local restaurants, where the native menus were unparalleled by any Spanish food we'd ever had in London. The same family owned all three restaurants and treated us like long-lost cousins. There was a full-moon party scheduled for later in the week, and the owner invited us along. His name was Marcus: a friendly guy, well groomed and fashionable. He explained that it was an annual event that attracted up to 300 people. There was no sound system, but everyone brought their own instruments to create an orchestrated jam. We gladly accepted the invitation and waited in anticipation for the night of the full moon.

The next day Glen took us to Sa Trincha, the semi-nudist beach at the far end of Salinas. It was home to the in-crowd, but much to my displeasure, most of the men were also naked, including Glen! I'd heard Ibiza could be eye-opening, but this was ridiculous! Sally convinced me to stay a little longer by promising to re-create one of my favourite fantasies. But I won't go into that!

I sat at the bar away from the naked men, buying everyone in sight a round of tequila slammers. The others left me to my own devices; they were far more interested in burning in the intense, harmful rays projected by the sun. Still, I met some really cool people and we spent the following hour buying one another more slammers. Before I got totally tilly-tallied, I left my Italian friends and returned to find Sally. I wasn't drunk, just slightly fizzed. Nevertheless, Sally laughed at the sight of me and asked if I minded her bathing nude. Call it insecurity or whatever, but I wasn't exactly cauliflowered on the idea – which didn't go down too well, either. Bluntly, Sally thought I was above such 'obsessive and chauvinistic' behaviour, and she pulled her sunglasses down over her eyes and lay back in disgust. I rolled two joints in silence, ordered a few beers at the bar and wandered off across the rocks along the coastline. Yeah, OK, maybe I was slightly out of order.

The salty breeze blowing up from the sea gently cleared my mind. It hit me like a church bell: I thought the world of Sally, and yet I had spoken to her in such harsh tones. Embarrassment wasn't the word, especially in front of close friends. I sat down by an old strategic defence post and gazed over the water. I didn't notice someone swimming my way until the naked man climbed out of the water, roughly 50 yards away. He waved at me but got no response, so he too sat on the rocks staring out to sea. While I was – for some reason – musing on the Spanish Armada, I could see the bloke edging closer and closer. Weirdly enough, he seemed to have his hands on his balls while stepping over the rocks. Then I suddenly noticed he had his erect dick in his mitt. Blimey!

I turned away in disbelief. There was no mistaking the fact that the man's actions were directed at me, because there was no one else around. With yards to spare, I erupted into an explosion of uncontrolled anger, leaving the man badly injured on the rocks. I'm not a violent person, but I don't like people coming at me tooled up, especially if that tool is a penis! Calmly I made my way back to Sally and the others, explaining that I wanted to go home for some quiet rest. Heika drove and told the others she'd return after a few hours to pick them all up.

When we reached the villa, Heika volunteered to rustle up some pasta. There was a bottle of JD in the cupboard, so we had a little snifter. Even with the doors and windows open, the rising temperature of the kitchen had us sweating shitloads. She asked if I minded her taking off the sarong wrapped around her perfect figure.

Don't you start! I thought, before telling her to go ahead. The silk material fell to the ground, leaving her naked, facing the cooker. The smile of a Cheshire cat bore no comparison to the smile on my cheeky mush, especially when she looked me straight in the eye and told me how sexy she thought I was. I returned the compliment, although I'm sure I stuttered with it. Heika was a well-known model in Germany, worshipped by corporate sponsors and agents alike.

She sat by my side, asking if I wanted to touch her. Honest, I'm not spinning no aubergenies here! It took every ounce of willpower in my body to stop myself. It wasn't rejection; I just felt loyal to Sally. If she'd walked in on us or managed to find out about it later, our relationship would have been chapatied. Maybe, if it had been a different place and she wasn't my girlfriend's brother's partner, things could have been different. As it was, I wasn't really tempted. Much.

We toasted our partners' health and were soon laughing again. She kissed me and went off for the others, who must have been black by now. Glen wanted us to go for a drink in his friend's bar, but I suspected it might be a bit warm to go into town so soon after bashing someone's head in! They left without me, while I sat by the pool having flashbacks of what had happened earlier. The guy deserved a lesson, but maybe hitting him with a boulder was a bit much. After years of non-violence, I really felt I'd let myself down. The worst thing was, I couldn't talk about it.

The next early morning was the full-moon party. Everybody was excited and did nothing but laze around by the pool during the day. The sun can have a funny effect on people: some scientists claim that the ionosphere and layers surrounding the earth's atmosphere work at much the same frequency as the human mind. Then, of course, there's the similar but not nearly as amenable notion of 'moon madness' . . .

Neatly, the party was staged at a secret location called 'Atlantis'. A centre for various hippie expeditions, it was said to be where several magnetic ley lines passing through the island crossed, giving Atlantis a reputation as the centre of Ibiza's spellbinding zest. It was also reckoned that a vortex above the island drew various energies from the cosmos, projecting a current directly on to the Balearics. Well, that's what Marcus reckoned anyway! It wasn't shown on any Johnny tourist map.

We arranged to meet Marcus outside the family restaurant. A convoy of 50 cars set off on the treacherous journey to Atlantis, or the 'Land of Oz', as many locals called it. A mountain range eclipsed Atlantis, which was based in a tiny bay at the bottom of the cliffs. The sight of burning beach fires and candles flickering in the wind and the faint sound of drums were unmistakable.

A trail of moving torch beams led the way down as people followed the yellow brick road. Becoming more excited by the minute, we soon reached the packed sand dunes, where hippies sat in large circles, singing while passing round various home-made bongs. About 30 drummers pounded their animal skins to the sound of African chanting. In another area, a consort of guitarists twanged away at strings and some girls with maracas joined in with percussion, complemented by the vocals of a Spanish cortège. Everyone else was on their feet dancing round the bonfires and up on the rocks overlooking the sea. In ten years of going to Ibiza, I'd never seen anything like it.

I'd taken some champagne and a bottle each of JD and tequila. Sally thought I was being greedy, because none of them wanted to drink alcohol. But everyone else was drinking, so why not join them? I sat with the drummers, offering the clansmen a choice of beverages, while Glen rushed the girls over to a clique of slick-looking queens. Time stood still as the starlit sky changed colour with every passing cloud. Suddenly, my Italian friends made a reappearance, the cue for us to continue where the last session had left off. Sally and the others were not too impressed, and eyed us from where their assemblage of queens with triangles were sitting. Heika, though, thought I was great fun and loved my sense of humour – as did most people, now that I mention it ... It seemed that Sally's and my relationship was going increasingly askew.

I stumbled off to relieve my flooded bladder, laughing to myself at the sound of chiming triangles and trying not to piss on my boots. But suddenly I felt a piercing pain in my head. Tiny bright blotches appeared in front of my eyes.

Then everything went black.

When I finally opened my eyes, I was shocked to find myself on the rocky deck, blood pouring from wounds in my forehead and the back of my skull. What the fuck had happened?

Claret stained what had once been a linen shirt. When my friends saw the state of me, they went mad and kept asking me what had happened. But I wasn't sure myself. Although I was pissed up, falling on to the rocks head first was not exactly my style. As I remembered it, the pain had arisen from the back of my head just before I'd passed out. Had someone clattered me?

Alex insisted on taking me to hospital, and went to tell Sally where we were going. But as we approached the circle, a familiar face in the crowd pointed at me. The face registered immediately: it was the man from Sa Trincha, the man whom I'd duffed up earlier!

He rose to his feet, surrounded by an angry mob. They ran straight at me, kicking and punching, sending my battered body into new, more powerful waves of pain.

Mercifully, when the Italians saw their new-found friend fighting for dear life, they came running in, fists first. In the confusion of who was fighting against whom, Glen got whacked a few times, so Sally started pulling this guy's hair. His girlfriend then attacked Sally, before I came to her rescue and pleaded for some calm. The Italians formed a rank around us both, in the confusion bashing Glen and all his friends. The party stopped whilst the mindless thuggery was taking place. Sally started screaming at me, 'Stay out of my life!'

I tried explaining that I'd been knocked out by the guy, but the damage was done. People lay on the floor in need of medical attention. Alex told me to forget her and go back to their place. Marcus couldn't believe it and wasn't at all happy, until I told him what had occurred. Course, I didn't tell him about the earlier incident, which was now preying on my mind like never before.

Alex took me to collect my stuff and promised me he had a woman back at the villa that most men would die for! He was right. Sally remained adamant that she wouldn't speak to me or even see me again, which bugged me, but at least there was the consolation of having met Sophia . . .

I briefly saw them all being dropped off at the airport by a swollen-faced Glen, but they ignored me. I left a few messages on Sally's answerphone in London, but got no reply. A few months later I bumped into a friend of her family, who explained that Glen, Heika and four others had sadly contracted Aids and were HIV-positive. I was horrified later to hear that all six died within twelve months (Sally moved to America and was never seen again). I would've made seven, but for a rare and unexpected display of tolerance, or perhaps a guardian angel was watching over me. That scared the shit out of me like nothing before in my whole life.

I only lasted a few months with Sophia, but still wouldn't dream of having unprotected sex.

# 21 Charlie Big Potatoes

In much the same way as drugs, alcohol has an adverse effect on some drinkers. A normally sensitive, caring, thoughtful and patient individual can turn out to be a right regular Jekyll and Hyde. Whilst pillheads hold hands and sing happy songs, pissheads are out the back having a punch-up. I mention this now because it leads me to the tale of Martin, which was a story told to me by someone at the Havin' It villa, in summer '95.

Martin exactly fitted the description of a violent drinker, but he preferred to blank everything out after a good night out. Most people agreed that he was a lovely fella, until the potent mixture of alcohol and drugs dissolved into his bloodstream. Once the toxins hit, he would become loud, arrogant and aggressive: drunk as a pirate on home leave, you'd think he didn't just own the gaff but had the world's entire back yard as his right of way.

For the most part Dutch courage aroused Martin's anger, making him so supremely confident that he'd confront anyone who looked at him. A fight could start at any time when he was on the bevvy. Most of his real friends learnt from past lessons and steered well clear when he'd had a few. The only people willing to back him up were the hooligans he was forced to knock around with. They'd pledged allegiance to the beer-soaked lone soldier and he did the same to them. It was a perfect, unholy alliance based on venom and destruction.

They'd bashed loads of people on the island already, and left a trail of nasty, vicious behaviour in their wake. The fact that they were undefeated so far gave them an air of supremacy and arrogance. Martin felt protected by this impregnable ring of steel, so he took even more liberties with everyone after a drink and had the recently acquired reputation of a true thug. Some of his mates carried weapons, including large kitchen knives, which they often used to chop the gear up with. None of them would hesitate for a moment when it came to the crunch.

As usual the evening began in a popular English pub in San Ann: tourists often flocked to the British boozer to watch the various televised sporting events. Martin was standing at the bar, shooting his mouth off, calling out orders to the intimidated staff. He snatched bottle after bottle from the bar and prised the lids off with his teeth. At one point he caught a ginger-headed bloke staring at him, and walked straight over to him.

'You got a problem?'

Ging apologised for looking at him, opening his mouth to reveal a set of horribly broken teeth. He'd damaged them days earlier, opening beers with his gnashers, and explained that was why he couldn't help watching Martin.

Martin frowned at the thought of crunching teeth – surprisingly, promising never to try it again. After leaving in a very drunken state, his gang latched on to some girls and followed them into another bar near the West End. Martin was pissed and desperate for a leak, so he hurried along to the bog to release excess water, after necking upwards of 20 pints of lager. The toilet was occupied and two others waited their turn. Impatiently he headed for the bar next door, where there was a much bigger cesspit. As he entered the bog, a group of Spanish mafioso types and their Latino señoritas were tooting powder off the sink unit. As Martin appeared, they stopped what they were doing and made him feel decidedly unwelcome. But Martin's water works were too far gone to be denied. With his back to the others, he simply whipped out Moby and thoroughly relieved himself.

'Hey, you,' came an aggravated voice behind him. 'What? You don't have respect for our ladies, you get your tiny dick out, like you were alone?'

Martin turned to face them. The entrance was blocked by a lump in a brightly coloured Versace shirt, which would have looked more at home in an art gallery than on someone's lumpy back.

'Señor,' replied Martin, 'if you had any respect for these ladies, they wouldn't be in a shit-house.'

Although cocky, Martin was in a no-win predicament. The guy calmly walked up to him, grabbed him by the hair and pressed the barrel of a gun into his nose. As he yelled at him in Spanish, Martin barely made out the part where he was being called an English pig. Even after all the lager, his transfixed expression told all. Fear paralysed his limbs, immobilising his ability to speak. The blackness of his pupils almost covered the green of his wide eyes.

'You English shit,' the Spaniard continued. 'Kiss my boot or I kill you.'

'Please, señor,' pleaded Martin uncharacteristically, because he knew he was in deep trouble. '*Qué pasa?*'

No sooner had the words fallen out of his mouth than a bottle smashed across his head, and the men started punching and kicking the big man as he lay crumpled on the floor, luckily managing to get himself into a ball so as to prevent really serious injury. After a few minutes they made a sharp exit.

Martin was shitting himself. He was convinced the whole bar was waiting to attack him. He said a silent prayer and stagger-ran out through the saloon into the street, where he puked his guts out until a few pals came over to help him. On hearing the news, they charged shouting into the bar, but the perpetrators had already left. Martin went home to sleep it off. This was not the end.

The next evening a detachment of warmongers went back to the Spanish bar with Martin, in the hope of finding the offenders. Anyone with a bit of common sense could feel the mood and temperament of the lads. They had their hands in their jackets and behind their backs as they tried to identify the local men. The barman turned the music down and asked them who they were searching for.

'Shut the fuck up,' came the rude response. 'Mind your own business.'

Resentfully they left the bar, making their way to the West End for a booze-up. It was about two in the morning as they returned 30-strong to the bar. They ran inside, expecting to find the Spaniards, but other than the same barman, there was no one else in sight.

'Tell your friends,' stated Barry, the team leader, 'we're coming back every fucking day until we find them.'

With that, Barry threw a bar stool at the barman, which missed and smashed into a large mirror behind the wooden bar, sending glittering fragments spinning into the cool night air. The barman kept his head low as the glass fell on to his body and the thugs headed for the door. The moment they left the exit, a torrential shower of bottles, glasses, tables, chairs, rocks and car parts rained down on the first one to hit the tarmac. The whole street lay in ambush and laid into the group, who were caught completely off their guard. A load of Spanish guys came running out of the toilets inside the bar and charged them from behind. This drove the thugs into the street, where it seemed that hundreds of Spanish people, both male and female, raged war against them. They were dramatically outnumbered and outmatched, and if the Guardia hadn't arrived fifteen minutes into the assault, someone would surely have been killed. The conflict continued at police headquarters, where the thugs were detained for hours before being allowed medical treatment. They were charged with a series of offences and given the opportunity to leave Ibiza and never return. Between them they had more stitches than a casualty ward in the East End, so they decided to accept the 'offer'.

The aftermath was ongoing. Martin suffered post-traumatic stress disorder from the ordeal, which has left him with a serious nervous disposition, including panic attacks whenever he thinks or sees anything violent. He subconsciously slips off into a mentally safe place where he cannot be harmed. Nowadays, he carries a small carved wooden dolphin everywhere he goes and swears blind that his life would end, if ever he lost the good-luck charm. Recently he spent a whole year in a mental institution, where as a born-again Christian he was eventually deemed fit to be released back into society. Nowadays, he continues to preach the word of the Lord and actively goes out recruiting and bringing Jesus into otherwise sad lives.

Some would call it a conversion. But me? I just call it karma.

# **22** Confessions of Famous DJs

Ever wondered about the lifestyle of a DJ? I bet you have, and I'd lay even more money that you've come back with a picture of something like this: high glamour, trunks full of cash, omnipresent business-class travel, pre-paid five-star accommodation, lovers in every venue, celebrity remixes, snogging and sniffing, the jetset, and nothing less than popstar status. All that palaver, and you'd be right.

Having said that, no DJ ever got where he is today without knowing a bit of hard work when it slipped under his decks. Honestly, when a DJ finally gets the credit he (or she) deserves, it shows how hard that DJ has grafted and pushed themselves to reach that platform.

Nowadays, DJs are usually bigger than the promoters and in some cases act as both. As an ex-party promoter myself, I've got some idea of the kind of attention a DJ receives from the adoring public ... especially the female (or male) groupies acquired at every gig. If you know what I mean.

The promoters set the stage, but it's down to the DJ to create the electrical atmosphere. No wonder they're the focus of everyone's attention, no matter what they look like (which is often just as well!). DJs have to read a crowd, manipulate their thinking and movement to suit the set, and take the punters to wondering heights. All that. That tune 'Last Night A DJ Saved My Life' says it all, although it certainly doesn't mention the whacking great fee!

I never wanted to be a DJ. No, really, I didn't. Then again, I have been behind the wheels of steel on a few occasions. My début set was played at one of my illegal Genesis raves (see *Class Of '88*) back in '89, when one of our own DJs got arrested en route to the warehouse. I played to 8,000 pilled-up fanatics that night, and they didn't give a toss if I could mix. I presume this means I was pretty good, but I wouldn't want to stretch the point if my reputation depended on it. My second shot was years later, in 1995, when I played a three-hour set to promote the 'Havin' It' in Ibiza CD at Pacha, now I remember it. And I still couldn't mix! Finally, later that year I held a short residency at the Soho Brasserie, in Sydney, Australia, where I played back to back. That was where I really experienced the power of a DJ at first hand.

A high percentage of women in the bar would, at some or other point in the evening, acknowledge me and the other DJ residents. Even if they were in the company of boyfriends or male companions, they'd secretly blow kisses. A few even slipped us their numbers while their partners were in the bogs. It was a sure-fire way of scorin' love *and* trouble! Course, the single women didn't give a damn and were even more upfront about it: cleavage showing, expressing mindful desires by wiggling their bodies in front of the DJ console . . . You know the jazz: fantastic!

Unsurprisingly, the female DJs always got a better reception than the males and sometimes almost caused a frenzy when on the decks. That's why I felt a few DJ confessions would be a lovely addition to my book – so long as I swore not to reveal their true identities, heh heh heh! See if you can guess who the culprits are!

### Look before you leap

Turntable Wizard (TW) joined the traffic as it slowed to a halt near the Egg in San Ann. He couldn't see any reason for the motors to stop and pulled out on the other side of the road to accelerate past the vehicles. When he reached the roundabout he realised why they'd stopped and slammed on the brakes. Like a vision from the heavens, two of the finest female specimens he'd ever clapped eyes on were strolling hand-in-hand along the beach front. Different guys approached the babes from all angles. Inevitably, the commotion attracted the Guardia Civil, who promptly moved the cars on and, by the looks of it, offered the goddesses a personal escort to wherever they were going. Typical Dib, but anyone would have thought a film star had just waltzed into town by the way everyone was acting. Even the other women were clocking the two chicks. The last time TW had seen such a fuss was when Linda Evangelista did a lingerie shoot on the streets of Ibiza Town. His temperature rose a degree or two just thinking about that one.

At Mambo's TW met up with some other top British DJs for a few bevvs. They'd all spotted the sexy chicks too, at different times and places over the last five days. None of them could mistake the hot tots and each promised to try their luck when they next came into sight: which, as it happens, was only five minutes after discussing it!

Flicking their wavy hair from side to side, the two girls entered the bar as if in slow motion, watched by TW. His DJ contemporaries were much more confident than TW himself, who wasn't the best-looking chap on the DJ circuit or even at Mambo's. They had all the girls after them and could just about serenade any woman they desired. TW had his fair share of crumpet, but was not in their league. The girls were immaculate, well-kept women, dressed from head to toe in Chanel, and immune to the bare-faced advances of the other punters. TW left his mates lining up to chat to them and went off to do some 'research'.

He sat down on the dimly lit rocks by the water's edge, and quietly took a small plastic bag from his pocket and sniffed two thin lines of gear. Following the snifter, he began preparing a nice skunk spliff that someone had given to him earlier. His hands were trembling, so he really had to concentrate on getting the joint together.

Suddenly there was a female American voice behind him.

'Hi. I know we haven't met before, but could you help us roll a joint?'

It was the girls ... Bells rang inside TW's head and a marching band played 'Summer Nights'.

'Yeah, sure, sit down,' he spluttered, amazed at his good luck.

They had high heels in their hands and wore pastel-coloured outfits, which revealed amazingly long, tanned legs.

'I'm Lana and this is Elena,' said one of them.

'My friends call me TW. Is this your first time in Ibiza?'

'Yeah, it's a pretty awesome place,' said Lana. 'We're going up to Ibiza Town. We don't get hassled as much as down here, so we'll have a couple of lines, smoke the joint and head back, I reckon.'

TW might not have been physically blessed, with looks, but he certainly had a sense of humour. He kept them laughing for ages, just by being his natural witty self. He should have been a comic, never mind a DJ. Soon enough, two of his DJ mates came over and immediately went in for the kill, by asking what the girls had planned for later that evening. Lana explained that TW was going to Ibiza Town with them and they'd decide what to do from there. Although he still couldn't quite believe it, TW took this in his stride, as he asked the girls if they were ready to leave. And so the threesome left arm-in-arm to the cheers and jeers of every geezer in the vicinity.

To top it off, TW was bang on form. Everything he said was perfectly executed and well appreciated. The women were at least five years his senior and were seemingly fairly wealthy. They bought nothing but the finest champagne in each bar they visited. Lana told him that money was no object and he should enjoy being spoiled for a change. Crikey. Had he died and been booked to play a set at Heaven?

Nah. Actually, TW was scheduled to play at Amnesia, so they drove down to the club. The two girls literally captivated the attention of both men and women. TW was feeling good, because the girls blatantly ignored everyone else, and he felt just massive. After inching their way across the heaving dance floor and climbing up into the DJ's platform, TW hit the decks.

His typically banging selection of happy house was enthusiastically absorbed by Amnesia's energetic clientele. Lana and Elena were performing their own dirty dancing, way above the admiring punters, who were delighted with the provocative dance routine. For two hours they wiggled and shook their arses to the rumbustious set of the Turntable Wizard. When he finished, both chicks gave him a lingering French kiss and recommended that they went somewhere more private. TW had them in the car park before their feet could touch the ground!

The girls were kissing and groping him as soon as they got into the motor. Lana had TW's manhood out in seconds and orally massaged the swelling flesh. He came instantly. The seduction was over. Brief, but as brilliant as half a ton of Dulux. The girls wanted to go home so that they could get up later that morning for some sun, so Lana told him to meet them the night before their departure. TW was euphoric. He couldn't wait to tell the lads about the night he was having. Full intercourse didn't bother him in the slightest, and he was happy to meet two days from then. Sex was guaranteed. Cor!

As expected, the others thought he had the right result, because they'd all tried it on and got absolutely nowhere. The hours couldn't pass quickly enough for TW and, on the night he planned to meet them, he scored some gear and put a few bottles of bubbly on ice. Incredibly, Lana and Elena looked even better than when he had first seen them. The deeply tanned beauties escorted him to a restaurant in the old town, where the threesome got merrily pissed and high on TW's supply. Some time later they almost fell through TW's apartment door, although funnily enough, the up-for-it DJ felt a little groggy, which was strange since he'd been caning loads of gear. It must have been the alcohol . . .

Elena stripped to her G-string and stockings, and shoved TW on to the bed. Lana produced a Polaroid camera from her bag and started taking pictures of Elena lying on top of TW. Immediately Elena returned the compliment by snapping her friend giving him a blow-job. Both women then joined him on the bed, where they performed – as the *Sun* would call it – 'a number of sex acts'! TW was barely conscious of what was happening and, soon enough, he fell asleep. When he awoke several hours later, the apartment was a total mess. Photographs depicting scenes of an explicit nature littered the bed and floor. He gathered them together and went to Mambo's to show the lads, where he almost caused a stampede showing the snaps to a captive audience of over 30 blokes. He gave the set to a fellow DJ to pass around the group. The DJ looked carefully at each snap before giving it to the next person in line. Suddenly laughter erupted and the DJ was screaming at the top of his voice.

## Spanish Highs

'It's a fucking geezer! TW has fucked another geezer!'
No way José!

With that, the fella bolted into the bar showing everyone his discovery. When he finally came to his senses, having already presented the bar with the mysterious picture, he came to TW, who was still sitting confidently in the same chair.

TW told them they were just jealous and that he should return the photograph, but the damning evidence was a photo of Lana and TW lying naked side by side on the bed. TW looked completely off it, while Lana had his dick in one hand and what resembled her own dick in the other. She had the tits and look of a woman, with a shaven set of balls! TW snatched the snap back, but the damage was thoroughly potatoed. Within days and maybe even hours the whole island, and London, knew of TW's misfortune. TW felt anger, sadness, betrayal and suicidal tendencies in the space of ten seconds. He left the bar at warp speed and touched down in London just days later, to find that his girlfriend of two years had cleared her stuff from his house, leaving him a note urging him not to call her. She also stated that she'd had an Aids test. He left for India the same week and didn't return until twelve months later. Dirtbox Syndrome stayed with him for a year after that, before he finally heard the last of it.

Well, until now, that is.

Sorry, mate, but next time look before you touch!

## DJ Lucky

Lucky had been DJ-ing for only a short amount of time. He'd jumped on the bandwagon after going to a few clubs and buying vinyl at trendy record stores. That's exactly how it starts for most modern bedroom DJs. First they go to all the gigs, then they compile tapes for their friends' recovery parties, which inevitably evolves into a set of decks, a mixer, cassette player and, before you can sing 'Something like a phenomenon', DJ Lucky is in the house.

OK, so his mixing skills needed fine-tuning – everyone has to start somewhere. He wasn't quite at rock bottom; more like first base. Lucky worked as hard as the next bloke and was determined to conquer the struggle towards excellence. At 21, he had bags of time to perfect his technique. The layman always landed on his feet and got booked regularly. So it was only a warm-up spot – exposure was what it was all about.

This was the first time the boys had been to such a crazy place and Lucky was loving every minute of it. There were thousands of bedroom DJs hoping to see their name in lasers, and he felt privileged to be booked in in the first place. Lucky's ambitions were fuelled by his love of music. Once his name was added to a club's playlist, he'd leave a burning building to get there on time. They could call him 24–7 and he'd drop the lot and make his way to the club. His commitment to his work was as strong as, if not even stronger than, his obligation to his wonderful girlfriend, who'd been at his side through the lows and endless struggles of his potential career. Like most aspiring DJs, Lucky's dream was to play live to an audience of more than 5,000 people. These objectives had yet to materialise, though, and this taunted his thoughts as he drove through the rocky hills of Es Canar en route to San Ann.

Suddenly, a scene straight from Lucky's wildest dreams appeared, in the shape of a red Ferrari, broken down by the roadside. In what was surely a blessing from the gods, the kaput vehicle had two very attractive angels sitting on its bonnet, waving frantically for his attention as his lower-grade rental Peugeot chugged towards them. The track was riddled with protruding rocks and muddy holes the size of a wheelbarrow, and Lucky knew that the flash car was dingered. The tall, upright women were Italian, but spoke perfect broken English. They'd somehow managed to perch the car on a big rock. The 100-grand motor lay wedged and couldn't move forward or backward without wrenching its chassis off. Eduarda and Romania had already tried and failed miserably. The car wouldn't budge.

They told Lucky that their home was a few miles away and asked him if he could take them there. Sure enough, the huge iron gates opened to reveal a large Spanish mansion with landscaped gardens and sculptured fountains.

'This house belongs to my boyfriend,' stated Eduarda. 'He's in Italy.'

'How did you get that car up and down the mountain without getting stuck before?' asked Lucky matily.

'Angelo will go crazy! When we are in Ibiza we drive the jeep,' answered Eduarda. 'But we wanted to drive the red car!'

She dialled a number from the house phone and began a conversation in her native tongue. Meanwhile, Romania popped open a bottle of Dom Perignon, pouring out three glasses.

'We drink,' she said, 'to DJ Lucky and the spirit of Ibiza, who bring this man to rescue us.'

Both women must have been in their mid-thirties, which slightly intimidated Lucky, but what the hell! The lad was enjoying himself. The B&O stereo piped Tracy Chapman throughout the villa. Eduarda told them that a tow-truck was on its way. They had a dinner date for eight o'clock and took the DJ upstairs to an enormous bedroom, where both women ran more or less naked around a large walk-in wardrobe until finally deciding what outfits they would wear.

It was apparently Eduarda's birthday a few days from then, so she invited Lucky to the party in her honour. He dropped them off near El Devino and continued on to the Café del Mar. Lucky couldn't believe his, well, luck! The women were very friendly, but to be honest he wasn't really sure if either of them fancied him or wanted to be his friend. Most of the girls he'd slept with (all four of them) had been younger than him and more impressionable. Eduarda and Romania had very strong personalities, touched with the fragile, feline quality of someone his own age. At the café no one believed him . . . they said he must be buzzing. One of the biggest moments in his life – and not a single soul would take his word for it. Bastards!

He held residence in a smallish club near the Egg in San Ann, which played banging commercial hits that got rinsed around most bars in the immediate vicinity. Its clientele consisted of scantily dressed girls in bright colours and likely lads in shiny shirts with big collars. When they drank it was purely to get trashed, leaving them systematically unconscious somewhere (roadside, club, beach, fountain, institution). The girls were very upfront but at the same time unattractive in their drunken stupors. It turned him off like a light bulb, that did. It wasn't so much what they said; it was more how they tried to do it. When pissed, the girls seemed to live out each emotion, and shoot from euphoria to downright depression. He did his set and went home for some rest.

Images of Romania and Eduarda faded into his dreamtime as he fantasised about being with Eduarda. Hours drifted by until the night of the party. Dutifully, he showed for work and left later than expected to reach the villa. The girls called him four times while in transit, expressing happiness and anxiety in anticipation of his arrival. They even purred what were unmistakably suggestive innuendoes.

He drove through the mansion gates and was surprised to find no other cars. Wondering if his car should be parked somewhere else, he stopped outside the front reception area. A voice over the intercom said to come straight in.

The stereo blasted raps with a hip-hop bass. Wearing tight hot-pants and tiny shrunk-to-size boob tubes, Eduarda and Romania came to greet Lucky, carrying a bottle of Crystal in each hand. Both kissed him passionately, before they led him into a large conservatory housing a swimming pool. The clear glass panels looked directly over the Mediterranean Sea. It was the picture of perfection.

Soon enough, though, Lucky realised that there was a distinct lack of other guests. Was the party simply, and amazingly, an excuse to get him there? The ladies were seductively drinking from the bottle, with their hands rubbing the insides of his legs. The conservatory was brought to life by loud giggling and what could have been the sound of children splashing about in the heated pool. Steam evaporated above the bubbles from the Jacuzzi as the threesome clambered into its white waters. Lucky's brain raced along at lightning speed: if only the lads who mocked the unknown DJ could see him now!

Naughtily, Eduarda put Lucky's hand on her full breast and slipped her tongue into his mouth. Lucky – nervous as hell – put the other hand on Romania's silicon implant. They exchanged pleasantries in Italian, then Eduarda reached for a large remote control, which opened several panels in the wall to reveal a pyramid of TV sets. All but the centre screen showed unadulterated porno movies, while the main screen showed a close-up of them in the Jacuzzi. The volume on all the sets was wired to the stereo and turned up to maximum. The grunts and groans of 20-odd people having sex simultaneously consumed every atom in the glorified glasshouse and transformed them into pulsating harmonics. Lucky's wildest imagination couldn't have conjured up this mating ritual. His initiation into manhood was about to be completed.

A unity of synergy and zest for natural pleasures sustained Lucky's performance. This, coupled with the amplified shrieks of the women throughout the household, somehow saw off the threat of a premature orgasm. But he still couldn't get over what was happening.

The flashing lights on his mobile phone beckoned for attention. Romania picked it up and answered the call.

It was Lucky's dad ringing from London to ask how he was doing . . . he'd left him the number. Lucky shared the moment with his father and fell about laughing. After expressing the urgency of safe sex, his father wished the youngster good luck and abruptly hung up. The demanding session fulfilled Lucky's most explicit hopes. In some countries what they did was punishable by criminal law!

The DJ could hold his head up high, as the women appeared satisfied by the young man just past the orthodox sexual peak of life. Their night ended on the roof terrace, with both women lovingly cradled under his arms. Hours later, he made some pathetic excuses and left the dumbstruck women at the house. He didn't have a prior engagement or anything: he just had to get away and tell somebody the news! Lucky had cracked it.

The guys took a bit of convincing, but finally rallied round believing the elaborate story. His phone was on 24 hours a day, awaiting that special call. A week later the women turned up at the club. The other astonished DJs squeezed into the DJ's box to witness the three greet one another. Yes, there were telltale signs of intimacy. Ear-to-ear whispers, and when both rich, well-bred chicks pushed their tongues into Lucky's mouth . . . blimey!

Romania told Lucky that someone had given them some sex tablets, which increase sexual pleasure. She held out the pills for his inspection.

'They're Ecstasy pills,' he confirmed. Neither of the ladies had ever taken drugs in their lives, so Lucky spent half an hour explaining E and its uses. He'd been caning pills every weekend for three years of his short life, so he was no stranger to the buzz. Still, he advised them to steer clear of the drug, because many tablets on the market were very dangerous. One bad one and their lives would never be the same.

They had a look of mischief in their eyes, then smiled at one another and popped two straight into their perfectly formed mouths, erupting into screams of laughter. Disappointed by their ignorant behaviour, Lucky had expected more from the adults. Even a teenager would have used a bit more common sense. Two straight Es for someone who'd never consumed an illegal drug was almost suicidal.

Half an hour later they were sitting down, dripping wet and completely out of their heads. Eduarda tried hard to reach the toilet, but puked over a group of clubbers clustered around a table. Two of the girls attacked her before Lucky reached the trouble-spot and pulled them apart. A guy came from nowhere, punching Lucky square on the chin and sending him flying over the table. Security came surging in and ejected the offenders from the premises, leaving the DJ and his mate nursing a few bruises. The women seemed unaware of the disturbance ... Eduarda kept asking why her face was marked. Romania suggested going back to the house. The Italians were in a mess, jawbones clattering together whilst their eyes twisted in their heads. It was getting embarrassing and Lucky had to get them out of there.

They stumbled towards the taxi rank, but Eduarda insisted on taking the super-car. She thrust the keys into Lucky's hand and ran towards the red devil. Two fuck-off-sized horns sprouted from above the headlights, pointed teeth with razor-sharp edges and spiked silver wheels. So, little boy, you want to PLAY! An almighty chariot worthy of the Prince of Darkness himself, thought Lucky; but he, being no angel, didn't fancy his own chances of handling it.

He pushed the button on the key pad, which turned off the alarm, unlocked the doors and, most startling of all, kick-started the powerful jet-propelled engine. Shaking his head, Lucky handed the keys back to Eduarda, who was kissing Romania. She threatened to drive herself if he wouldn't do it.

Eduarda sat back in the leather upholstery, while Romi knelt on the floor facing her friend. Although the gears were quite close together and the accelerator slightly hard, Lucky drove the car like a natural.

The women were too preoccupied with one another even to notice that the vehicle was in motion. Now butt-naked, they gently massaged their bodies, oblivious to the peering eyes from passing vehicles. Glancing constantly in the rear-view mirror, Lucky manoeuvred the Ferrari around the tricky dirt track to the house. Immediately their attention turned to him. Both were savagely ripping at his clothes, positioning his body where they could get to him easily. Some time later they went inside. Romania opened a litre bottle of vodka, swallowing at least one-third of the bottle, then passed it to Eduarda. Lucky hated the transparent fluid, but necked the alcohol just the same. The Italians, diehard in their approach, begged him to spank and rough them up a little. He obliged, but felt rather uneasy.

The carnage must have looked more aggressive than sexual, as both women yelped with pleasure and struck back with force. Lucky wondered if they always acted so violently when having sex, or if the effects of the MDMA had driven them beyond their own personalities. Coupled with the intoxicating effect of the vodka, the women were not only stronger than him, but black, blue and yellow lumps had already appeared over their anatomy. The session went on: bondage, Lucky being tied to the bed, and – much to his distaste – Eduarda shoving the remaining two pills down his throat while she held on to his nostrils.

Lucky choked and pleaded for mercy, but they left him blindfolded in the dark room while chasing one another round the house. The buzz came from the back of his head, moving between his neurones and hiding behind memories. A half-hour could've been an hour – he didn't have a clue.

While he was rushing, he suddenly realised that someone – Eduarda – was sitting on top of him. He couldn't see it, but she was holding a burning candle in each hand. Romania stuffed a tangerine into his mouth to stop him shouting. A beam of light flickered on and off in his face before they ripped the blindfold off.

The chemically processed women had the vacant glint of two

persons not entirely in control of their own actions. A momentary bout of pain ended as fiercely as it began. 'Firestarter' drowned out Lucky's muffled cries, as wax poured on to his legs, arms, chest and, most excruciating of all, his balls. He no longer wanted to play their game; even the E-rush was turning into a bad trip.

With him stranded there, Eduarda appeared from another room and lashed him across the chest with a leather whip. It hurt like fuck. The juice from the tangerine crushed in his mouth was now blocking his airwaves. Romi scooped the chunks from his mush, slapping him hard in the face, and Lucky went berserk, hurling all manner of abuse at them. He told the hysterical witches he would torture them both, which merely seemed to please them even more.

They gagged him with a stocking, fastening another blindfold across his eyes again. Sharp teeth broke the skin surface of his leg and chest. Into his mind came images depicting premonitions of being eaten alive by the world's most beautiful cannibals. He could see the tree tops and light breaking through the branches above the growling faces at the heart of this feeding frenzy. Unable to move, scream, struggle or escape, he sent an urgent message to God, pleading for forgiveness and help, although he wasn't even religious. Nothing happened for a few moments, until suddenly the rays of sunlight burst intrusively through the trees and devoured the grotesque faces. Good had conquered evil. DJ Lucky had passed out.

He awoke hours, or maybe even days, later, strapped to the die-cast metal bed. The linen was drenched and the sun shone directly on to his weary body. Cuts and abrasions fired stinging ripples from head to foot. But a burning internal anger was replaced by a chilling fear. Held captive the entire night, he felt like a prisoner rather than someone having a sexual experience. On the other hand, he felt the almost subconscious, but unmistakable and undeniable twitch of pleasure.

A loud, piercing scream almost ruptured his eardrums and he heard footsteps running away. Left alone with nothing but his thoughts, he wondered if the women had come down from the drugs and realised what they'd done to their toy boy. But if that was the case, why the fuck didn't they untie him?

Around half an hour later he heard footsteps and voices heading towards the room. The door crashed against the wall and a flurry of Spanish male voices filled the void. His blindfold and gag were removed and, after he'd adjusted his focus to the sunshine, the figures standing over him transformed into Guardia Civil. They shouted at the youngster but they didn't understand English.

The irate voice of Eduarda engulfed the room. The officers stood to attention while she ripped into them in Spanish, waving her fingers in the captain's face and yelling at the maid standing next to them. Lucky could only imagine what she was saying, but it wasn't too hard to get his head around it. Even as an empty shell, the house must be worth millions – her boyfriend Angelo had to be minted. Money is power, no matter who's paying, and Eduarda sent the officers packing in no time, then untied Lucky. Immediately he grabbed her by the throat, throwing her down on to the bed and squeezing her air tubes. She didn't try to resist, but glared into his eyes as he choked her to certain death.

CRACK!! Broken glass fell on to Lucky's face and shoulders, leaving him temporarily stunned, before falling into blackness. He regained consciousness in hospital nursing a serious headache, and smothered in bandages. The doctor told Lucky that he had been brought in by a woman in a red sports car, who said she found him on the roadside. They were curious how the youth had managed to get into such a state. There was a six-inch gash needing twenty stitches and an inventory of other injuries. The alcohol level in his bloodstream led the medics to assume he'd been fighting.

Lucky checked out of hospital and went home. Being unable to work for a few days, some of his mates came to the apartment and found him looking battered. They got a firm together and went back to the villa. A male Italian voice brought the tiny electrical box and camera mounted on the outside wall to life. They demanded to speak to Eduarda and Romi. After a few minutes the gates opened, so they casually strolled up the drive towards the house. Six different sports cars were parked in front of the reception area, from where three men came out of the house with angry expressions on their faces. One of them held a big knife. The lads turned and ran for the gate, not knowing why the fuck they were running. The men gave chase, picking rocks up in the garden and throwing them at the group. After reaching their cars safely, the retreating army left more quickly than they had arrived. Off, off and away.

Lucky called a meet with a load of San Antonio's workers on the strip. Peezy and Blocko were driving past and noticed the gathering. Lucky told his heroes the score and hoped the duo would come along, but the DJs were rolling up. Finally, Peezy issued a serious warning about going against the Italians, because apparently Angelo was a fully fledged mobster. The would-be avengers dispersed immediately. Lucky tried to stop his loyal pals, but they would have none of it. Peezy and Blocko knew the Italians, through mutual friends who'd asked the DJs to play in a large club in Italy. They advised the rookie to heed their warning, so he took their advice as a sign that he should leave Ibiza, and returned with his tail between his legs to his trusting girlfriend.

Shortly after touching down at Gatwick in the early hours, Lucky went straight to her place and found the missus in bed with one of his best mates.

But hey! Don't even go there!

## DJ Sniper

Antarctic winds ripped through the rainfall, blowing freezing cold water straight into Sniper's face. The dealer he'd arranged to meet was fifteen minutes late and the DJ was totally pissed off with her. Nothing had gone right lately. The lad was banned from driving for five years, which meant he got cabs everywhere, except at weekends when he'd hire a driver. He was meeting one of the most glamorous drug dealers in the world . . . but outside Camden Town tube station?

He'd learnt years ago to keep his valid suppliers close to heart by not allowing anyone to see or even know the distributor's identity. These being the nineties, drug dealers no longer fell into easily recognisable stereotypes – if they ever did.

Linda had dated popstars, eastern princes, heads of international cartels, politicians, trust-fund wild childs and female models. Hardened by four years' imprisonment in Asia for keeping her mouth shut and not spilling the beans on her kingpin boyfriends, this had only made her even more attractive, more forceful. Not many males could resist such individuality and they always fell under her spell.

Sniper had met Linda in Space, hitting it off instantly. The chance platonic relationship had grown beyond their expectations and the pair grew to love one another in a brother-sister kinda way. Her current partner was someone high-ranked in Holland and ran a multinational team of dealers. He'd known about Sniper from the off, but put him down as more of a faggot than the ladykiller he actually was!

On the other hand, Sniper wasn't looking for anything more than friendship. Linda really looked after him when it came to supplying drugs. If her fella found out she'd been redistributing his stock, without declaring her actions, he'd have done his bollocks. Linda's role in the flying Dutchman's flourishing business was officially non-existent, and he never discussed his daily routines in front of her. Still, several of his 'employees' would often try to pull her, a slip that Linda would use against them in the form of blackmail, with threats to tell the Dutchman traded against supplies of hard drugs.

Whenever Sniper needed stocks, she'd send one of the guys round with everything he wanted at rock-bottom prices. He shivered when at last a Porsche stopped outside the station; he jumped into Linda's dream machine and sped off at high speed. She gave the DJ all he required before dropping him home and returning to the Dutchman, who was preparing to leave for Argentina. Sniper packed his clothes and records before getting a cab to Lee's, where he met up with the others.

Lee and Tony were upstairs, discussing how to smuggle drugs into the Balearics. The supplies belonged to the three of them, so it was left to the Brady Bunch to carry the stash through customs at Gatwick. It was usually a simple procedure: just stuff the bags down yer shorts, no problem. Well, except for one major flaw.

The normally low-profile customs at Evissa had been randomly picking tourists from the baggage hall and giving the nominees a strip-search. At least ten people had been arrested in the past six weeks, which by Balearic standards was alarming. The smugglers needed to be extra careful and not take anything for granted. Lee made an executive decision. He drove to the nearest petrol station and brought ten chocolate Kinder Surprises. The tiny, round plastic container inside the egg was deemed a perfect size to stash their goods and shove up their anal passages.

'WHAT?!!!!' choked Sniper. 'Are you fucking mad? There's no way on earth I'm sticking two eggs up my arse, mate. You must be off your nut.'

'I don't fancy shoving them up my arsehole, either, but this ain't about pride; it's about staying out of a foreign prison,' snapped Lee. 'If you're coming with us, you've got to plug, otherwise what's the point in any of us plugging? I'm not being funny, Sniper, but you're more likely to get stopped than any of us. Look at yourself. You've got long hair and you're carrying a record box into Ibiza! It's no big thing. What's the matter with you?'

They had to be at Gatwick soon, so there wasn't time to argue, although Sniper did his best.

'No big deal, what do you mean no big deal? You're trying to convince me to shove two plastic eggs up my arse because I've got long hair and a record box! I'm not doing it.'

Sniper hadn't had so much as a finger poked up his bum in the heat of passion, so the thought of travelling abroad with egg-like containers measuring close to three inches long was absolutely mind-numbing.

An ounce each of Latino disco dust, super-skunk 12 and a hundred pills were stuffed into the airtight eggs. The colour-coordinated capsules were then thrown on to the bed. The lads chose two each and one by one went into the bathroom, Vaseline in hand, and plugged.

Lovely.

Sniper thought the lads did have a point: customs had made a few surprising dawn raids on holidaymakers from the UK. Grimly, he eventually entered the bathroom, lubricant in hand, but after reviewing his predicament he made a bold decision that he'd rather go to prison than break his rear virginity. In ten years of going to Ibiza, he'd never once been stopped or even seen anyone else get tugged. He pinned the eggs to the underside of his shorts and told the others he'd plugged. They loaded their cases into the cabs and made their way to Gatwick.

The six-hour door-to-door journey was uneventful, and before long they were toasting their arrival in the hotel's bar. A bottle of vodka was rapidly necked, until Sniper came to realise that the other guys still had the Kinders up their dirtboxes. He watched in amazement as both Tony and Lee insisted on drinking another bottle. So they did. During the fast-streaming banter, amongst the laughter and over the sound of music could be heard the words of . . . judgement.

'Oi! How comes you haven't unplugged yet?'

The taunt had a delayed reaction, which began as a giggle and ended in pain, rolling around the floor. They were in bits. Sniper knew the boys were bona fide, but it did take some explaining. I mean, to be honest, what heterosexual male wouldn't remember to remove plastic containers from his jackse?! They both vanished and returned clutching the narcotic Fabergés. Tony, Lee and the others left Sniper at the hotel, whilst they went on to Mambo's.

The DJ was almost addicted to self-abuse, whether it was drugs, alcohol or personal relationships. Leaving their stash under Sniper's supervision was barmy: the lad just couldn't help himself. One up the hooter, all up the hooter . . . there was no difference to him. He set four trench-like lines on top of a record sleeve.

Sniper, like thousands of other persistent coke users, has the same trip each time he sniffs plenty. The buzz begins chatty, then the tiger makes a grab for his tongue, allowing him time to reassess his life, rendering the left side of the brain in a state of anxiety, fear, panic, insecurity and isolation. He decided to catch up with his pals at the bar.

As he walked through the corridor, the sounds of people in their rooms grew louder, until a door opened and two girls nearly knocked him to the ground. Wired, Sniper jumped back in shock into a wall, causing a picture to fall and break on the shagpile carpet. All three screamed. Sniper was overcome with embarrassment and rushed back to his room, locking himself in and listening behind the door. The girls thought Sniper acted bizarrely, but so does everyone in Ibiza, so they weren't at all concerned. The corridor lay silent and still, as the DJ stood by the door for more than an hour, pausing only to sniff a few more lines.

Suddenly, the quiet corridor erupted into life. Voices, loud and boisterous, came to a halt outside his room. Bang, bang, bang! The noise freaked him out, so he ran into the bathroom to avoid being discovered.

'Hey, Sniper! Open the door, you fucking twat,' said a voice he recognised. It was Scouse Paul.

'Get a move on, will ya?'

A relieved Sniper let his mates into the room and asked if anyone had seen them walking down the corridor. They looked at one another and laughed. 'What's up, kiddo?' joined Walshy. 'Someone out to get ya, yer paranoid cunt!'

Paul invited Sniper for a few beers back at his villa, but Sniper wasn't in the mood. They jibed the DJ until he agreed to go with them and bring some supplies. But, walking from the hotel, his paranoia was raging. As he headed for the taxi rank by the sea front, a geezer wearing a polo shirt, blue jeans and white trainers said hello.

Sniper told him to 'Fuck right off', which the others found hilarious.

The packed streets were bulging with various bars integrating their atmospheres. Sniper counted exactly 20 polo shirts in one concentrated space. Watching them not watching him, he jumped into the waiting vehicle.

It didn't take long to reach the villa. A few women were already there and dancing in bikinis to loud music. They joined the party, soon forgetting Sniper's weird antics, and sniffed some more gear. Lots more.

When the horrors returned hours later, Sniper decided to go back to the hotel. There was no phone at the villa, so he had to walk through pitch blackness until reaching the road lights, in the hope that a taxi would pass en route to town. He could hear the crickets at it in the night. He liked their approach to shagging. Wham bam. Thank you. Fuck off!

Footsteps behind him in the distance brought the anxiety back with a vengeance, and his heart skipped the second beat.

He increased his stride almost to a trot, but could hear the footsteps running after him. Sniper legged it all the way to the hotel. He passed two guys sitting in a motor at the end of the road and another Dodge vehicle containing two big lumps, parked directly opposite his balcony. The reception was quite busy for three in the morning, and two suited bodybuilders stood next to the main desk. This wasn't an unusual sight, because most hotels and apartment blocks had security guards to stop non-residents from entering the premises or to eject the unruly. But their presence unnerved Sniper. As he passed the concierge's desk, a uniformed member of staff asked if he'd had a good night. Acknowledging this with a grunt, he scarpered upstairs to the second floor and into more rampant psychological disturbance.

How did he know my name? thought Sniper. I can't remember seeing him before!

He left the lights off, but still closed the curtains and sat down in a chair near the door. Waiting, listening for movement.

Who were the guys in matching uniforms? The torture continued. There must be a connection.

Lee and Tony had come and gone already, leaving the place in a right mess. An hour passed: Sniper hadn't moved a muscle, not even for a line. The buzz was coming down, making it easier to control the voices inside his mind. He was reclaiming his sanity, snatching it back. It worked. The mental battle had been won, and to celebrate his feat he unscrewed the end of the room's brass curtain rail and pulled out three bags hidden inside the tube. A piece of string came out with the last bag, so he yanked it and felt something tied to the other end. A long, thin, sausage-shaped transparent wrapper revealed a brown powder substance, which he immediately recognised as heroin, or curry powder! Sniper had seen smack in the past, but had steered clear and never wanted to try it. What the fuck was it doing here?

He'd done most of the media-labelled 'designer drugs', but scag appealed to a different circle: people not too bothered about looking like death warmed up. Admittedly, back in the eighties, Sniper had been given the nickname 'Pop-eye' for his prodigious use of Ecstasy, but the similarities ended there. From what he knew of his business partners and friends, neither would trade in smack. He took the medicine bags into the bathroom and chopped up some Charlie on the ceramics. A tiny light for shaving was barely enough for him to see what he was doing.

Suddenly the phone rang as he was about to sniff, causing him to blow the roughly formed lines and some of the bags' contents into the bath. He panicked, running from the bathroom into the bedroom several times, before remembering the drugs attaché on the floor. Scraping what was left of the coke back into the bag, he tried stuffing the gear back whence it originally came. The heroin bag was now out of its original shape, having burst under the pressure and covered his hands, face and chest area. The phone stopped ringing. His throat throbbed and particles enraged the fading senses in his nostrils. He needed to cough, sneeze or shout out in discomfort. Glued to the spot, and not wanting to make a sound, he decided to make his move before he was toasted. Like a Riverdancer, Sniper sprang into the bathroom coughing his heart out, while trying to wash the shit off his body. He still felt dirty, so he jumped under a freezing cold shower for nearly a minute, before taking his wet clothes off. He quickly changed into another summer outfit and carried on the task of cleaning the evidence. It took the best part of an hour to wedge the gear carefully back into the brass tube. When he'd finally done it, he was much more relaxed. Surely his friends would understand and would not hold it against him? It was a simple accident brought on by the fear of being arrested. No one could expect any other reaction from someone who thought the game was up.

Sniper's bouts of paranoia were almost stabilised, so he gave in to the urge to sit out on the balcony. His skin was irritating – he kept scratching. Then he noticed his slow heartbeat – unlike the effect of coke, which speeds the ticker. His eyelids were like lead weights, which made him feel tired but still wide awake. Without warning he puked over the balcony. Although unpleasant to the eye, this sudden regurgitation had a pleasant after-rush that made him feel light-headed. He lay on the sun lounger, examining the stars, thinking about friends back in London. Looking down at the road below, he observed what he thought was a person crouched behind a dark-coloured vehicle.

Is that someone spying on me?

He'd have sworn on oath that the man was looking straight up at him. The DJ pretended not to have seen him and continued monitoring the sky, but Sniper had his number. He had on a dark uniform of some sort. Leaning on the rail, Sniper looked up and down the road as if expecting visitors, but really it was to get a clearer view of the other two vehicles.

That's got to be Guardia Civil.

He stretched out his arms in a yawning gesture and walked back inside, closing the curtains behind him. He grabbed some personal effects, along with his passport and toothbrush. The telephone ringing got him every time, like a bullet slicing through the surrounding matter and reaching its target. It stopped his advance towards the door with a shudder, as he imagined the worst about to happen. Back out on the balcony, Sniper noticed that the man was still in exactly the same position as when he had first seen him, ages ago.

What was going on?

Secretly Sniper pictured an army of non-English-speaking fatigues running up the hotel stairs, riding the lifts, blocking all escape exits. He saw an indigenous judge looking down from the bench with disgust, after seeing local children addicted to smack, and wanting to send a golden flare to potential British smugglers. In his mind, he heard the judge give him ten years and then saw a humid, cockroach-enriched prison cell shared with a block of nationals only too willing to bash an Englishman's head in.

Fuck that!

He wrenched the tulip off the brass rail and gently pulled the drugs stash from the tube. He rushed into the bathroom, pouring the brown and white powder down the pan. Then he crumbled the Es into powder as best he could and did the same with that. The super-skunk 12 was broken down and wrapped in toilet paper, and also flushed into the sewer system. Sniper rinsed his face with cold water and pulled himself together. That was it, nothing illegal in the gaff.

His confidence rejuvenated, he decided to search for his mates and warn them of the dangers, so he bowled out of the building, past the hidden eyes.

He searched the bars for hours before finding one of his travelling companions. She said they'd just gone back to the hotel with a few Liverpudlian lads. Sniper told her there was no time to explain, but advised her not to go back to the hotel for at least 24 hours. Then came a quick dash back to the hotel, past the observing vehicles and through reception. He burst into the suite, where everyone jumped with fright. One of the strangers was standing next to the door when he came in and grabbed Sniper by the face, slamming him against the wall.

'What you fucking playing at, cunt? Can't you walk into the room like a normal person?'

'Forget that!' interrupted Lee. 'Where you hidden the gear?'

'Hey,' the even meaner-looking Scouser accused Sniper. 'Do I know you? Can you tell me how come a stranger has touched my fucking gear? You see, that brown, it belongs to me. Now where is it?'

As Sniper heard Lee call the man 'Spanner', fear seeped into his soul. He recognised the notorious name from stories told by his Scouse pals back home. Spanner, he remembered, had broken out of prison twelve months previously after serving fifteen years of an indefinite sentence for murder. Her Majesty's Pleasure (HMP) is a punishment sentence for young offenders and in some cases is an even stiffer sentence than life. Every five or ten years a review board representing Crown and country has a quick overhaul of the prisoner's crime and the rehabilitation, whilst also assessing his good behaviour and remorse.

Spanner was a savage skinhead at the time of the crime, hooked on the glue-sniffing craze that rocked Britain's more deprived youth. A violent fucker, too, and time behind bars had done nothing but increase his destructive attributes. Fifteen years on, a lost teenager had become a ruthless, unemotional, self-satisfying man: a right bastard.

Sniper told them the whole story and took the angry mobsters out on to the balcony, pointing to the man and the guys in both vehicles. But there was no one there, or at least none could see what Sniper saw.

Tony, in a desperate attempt to stand by his mate, even went downstairs to take a closer look. He stood in the exact spot where Sniper had seen the man. Nothing – nor in the vehicles. Sniper was in deep shit.

Spanner whacked him with his nemesis – that fucking telephone.

Tony tried breaking it up, but all three partners were huddled together as if about to face a firing squad. In reality they were.

'Do ya think I'm fucking daft or what?' fired Spanner. 'I want the smack or the money for five ounces. I'm not kidding you, Tony. It was your idea to leave it here in the first place. I want it right now, or I'll cut you wide open, you fucking cunt.'

Sniper, Tony and Lee pleaded with Spanner to believe the story. They were taken to a villa near San Antonio and roughed up a little. Spanner's friends promised to keep Sniper prisoner until he paid back every cent. The DJ barely scraped together his share of their own drugs kitty: he certainly didn't know anyone who'd lend him four and a half grand. The Scousers let Tony and Lee free, whilst confining Sniper to a windowless broom cupboard.

His friends didn't know what to do or who to call for help. Tony then found Linda's address and private number on a postcard list in Sniper's bag. Although they'd never been introduced, their pal spoke very highly of the kingpin's missus and they knew she was kosher. She'd help out, or at least inject some new ideas, because they were clean out.

Tony rang the mobile. He told Linda everything while she clung on to every word, but when he'd finished she went ballistic. Why'd they left their friend with the murderer in the first place? What were they – sissies?

'Whatever your friends do to Sniper,' she promised, 'I do to you. Now, go back to the hotel and wait for my friends to contact you. If anything happens, make sure you call straight away.' Click.

'What a bitch!' retorted Tony, but they were soon staring at the patterned wallpaper of their suite. The Scouse firm rang them every half an hour, repeating their threats. So when would Linda's friends get there? Hours? Days?

Someone knocked on the door hours later. It was Monday, and everyone was at Manumission, so apart from the goon squad, no one was expected. Surely it couldn't be them?

Tony opened the door to be confronted by Spanner's mates, the Toxteth Massive. Six of them piled into the suite and the ringleader did his Al Capone bit. Tony reassured them that the payment was practically en route from Holland and would be there promptly. But the Toxteth Massive needed the money there and then – not excuses or promises.

Tony suggested calling their friend to find out what was delaying things. He thanked God the phone was on and that Linda answered. He told her the debt collectors were present and keen to recover the lost funds. She asked to speak to the main guy, and told him the money was coming by ferry from Barcelona and would be there the following day. The Scouser threatened Sniper's life, then hung up.

At that precise moment someone knocked on the door and one of the lads opened it. The hallway was crammed with bodies. At the head of the pack stood a short, stocky Spanish dude who asked if Tony or Lee was home.

'Yeah, that's us,' said a voice behind the six geezers.

The northern laddie who had been doing the talking launched himself across the bed, grabbing hold of the bloke on Lee, and holding a knife to his throat.

'What the fuck's going on?'

Without speaking a word, four of the men calmly pulled their arms from behind their backs to reveal a variety of handguns.

'You know, my friend,' said the Spaniard, 'this can be resolved without any blood loss. We are here to liberate the DJ. If we can do this without trouble, it's better for you. But first let me tell you that I was born here in Ibiza and if something goes wrong today, I will still find your Spanner and also the DJ within hours. So, my friends, do the right thing, OK?'

One knife dropped to the floor, then another, until all the weapons were on the deck. The Spaniard spoke some German, signalling one of the others to pick the cutlery up. Lee and Tony tried thanking him, but they got told to shut up and explain where Sniper was being held.

Spanner and his friends had a large villa five minutes from the Kanya Bar. The Scousers were duly bound and gagged with sheets, pillowcases and net curtains. The Spaniard asked for Sniper's passport and belongings. One man and his gun watched the prisoners while the others rushed to the rescue. The plan was simple enough: snatch Sniper at gunpoint and, if this Spanner bloke tries to stop them, he gets his head blown off.

As soon as they arrived outside the villa, two Germans moved swiftly into action and scaled the surrounding wall before the Spaniard had even got out of his car. Within seconds, the main gates opened and the gun-toting slingers waltzed into the grounds. Spanner and his lads were fast asleep in cuckoo land. They woke with a jolt and six inches of steel in their faces.

They found Sniper in the cupboard, with minor cuts and bruises, but really glad to be free. Before they left the astonished Scouser group, all their suitcases were searched and anything with a name and address printed on, including passports, was taken as security against repercussions. Spanner was livid, but even a fool could see that his lot were outmanned, not to mention outgunned. The Spaniard said that Sniper would be leaving for Barcelona the following day, where he'd meet someone who would drive him to Marseilles in time for the flight to Holland.

Lee and Tony were advised to watch their backs, whilst the mesmerised DJ was whisked away. Linda was on hand to collect him by limo and take him briefly to her massive house, while the bigwig kingpin was in Argentina on cartel business. He loved the house and seriously considered going after a taste of the dream, but Linda advised against it. He'd never have made a big-time drug dealer, even before his recent 'difficulties'.

He stayed in Holland for a week before returning home to London. Tony and Lee were already back from Ibiza, unhurt and full of beans. Linda called days later to say that her boyfriend had been shot dead in Argentina and she was off to collect the body.

Sniper's dream shattered immediately. Lee and Tony agreed never to smuggle or sell drugs again . . . And Sniper?

He learnt to stick to playing records. Heard the one about a Massive Attack?

# 23 Jimbo's Birthday

There was a lot of excitement at the Havin' It villa in the late summer of '95.

There was an annual pilgrimage attracting near on 200 mad-for-it crusaders. Jimbo was a *Class Of '88* veteran, who understood full well the concept of week-long clubbing sessions. In other words, he was a bit bananas! As a party promoter in the early nineties, Jimbo'd held residency at the Astoria for a couple of years. Back in that day, he'd also presented a number of club events on this very island. Nowadays, though, his fingers were in all sorts of pies, and the only time you'd see him in a club was when he was up for a right nutty night out. It was never something he'd pre-arrange: as with most clubbers, his most wild nights arose out of an impulsive decision that he'd often regret later.

The specially selected guests for his birthday bash were hardcore warhorses, who were promoters, DJs, club hosts, celebrities, sports personalities, models, brokers, estate agents, millionaires, boys from the hood and all manner of similar social detritus. God knows how, but they were the sort of people who could all manage to hold down a daily routine or job whilst maintaining a turbo-charged lifestyle. And I ain't talking about their motors (although there were usually plenty of good 'uns knocking about). No, I mean a rollercoaster diet of drugs, sex, money and long drawn-out weeks . . . in that particular order. The odd sports star aside, fewer than 10 per cent of them had been within 20 yards of a gym or a healthy balanced diet. Fuck that! Alcohol and drugs obliterate the urge to eat anyway, so until one of them collapsed from debilitation they'd get right at it. Come to think of it, even if one of them did pass out, they'd carry on anyway!

## Spanish Highs

Ibiza's two main high points of the year were – and are – the beginning and the end of each punishing season. The legendary birthday bash coincided with September, when most of the dizzy workers and Johnny Tourists were fighting with the elements in the UK. But not in Ibiza. Each sun-soaked September would climax in a wild, extravagant, eccentric, imaginative and unfeasibly grandiose presentation of the world's most infamous party circuit. For the best part of the year (apart from people from non-English-speaking countries), Ibiza is usually swamped with youngsters from the regions outside London, stretching as far and as remote as the highlands of Bonnie Scotland right down to Canvey Island.

A lot of Jimbo's pals were Londoners and, for the only spell in four months, the hot spots around the island were besieged with Cockney geezers. Not the 'Wot, you want some?' types at all – not by a long shot – but a more confident, stylish bunch of entrepreneurs from the cream of England's clubland. Old school, matey. There were also a considerable crop of madcap northern promoters, which meant that the whole thing was like a top-level dance summit with a side-order of hedonism.

The thing that always confused me was how these participants – not all of whom were overly familiar with each other – always seemed to follow a certain regime or methodical cycle, nearly always ending up at the same places, even if at different times. Nobody knew quite how it happened, but it was as if they were drawn by some irresistible force or code. Actually, if I think about it, perhaps this is where the Chaos Theory started! But, now that I think about it, this was *total* chaos, and there wasn't a lot of theory going down. Half the time few of 'em could even talk!

I suppose someone, somewhere must have been pushing the right buttons, organising the guest list or having a quiet word with the club owners. Fuck knows who, or how they got there in the beginning. Anyway, the excursion started at a dinner for at least a hundred people (the other guests tended to skip their food and sniff their own dessert). An exclusive five-star resort was the selected venue for a number of years. This hotel complex was by far the most luxurious on the island, and was often peopled by a league of superstars who'd been coming for nearly two decades. Name them, they'll have been there. Unlike some of Ibiza's more conventional hotels, which resemble fancy council blocks, this resort was a labyrinth of self-contained lodges set in a hill overlooking Ibiza Town and San Antonio. The owner personally saw to it that all guests were treated like royalty, and privacy was paramount. It was a total relaxation experience that entrapped good karma and inspired many an artist.

Apart from rock 'n' roll stars, the management was not too keen on people throwing parties. However, Jim and a lot of his guests had been staying there on and off for over thirteen years. Jimmy had become good friends with the owner and the respect was mutual: which was just as well, because if the latter knew the amount of class-As sitting round every table, he'd have closed the gaff down! But that night he rarely made an appearance and certainly didn't have a clue what was going on. Not that anyone took the piss: all the drug-taking was strictly cloak-and-dagger, or, more literally, cloak and bog cubicle!

The stash of stuff going down (or up, if we're talking noses) read like a smuggler's haul. Two kilos of Peruvian marching powder, 3,000 pills, 100 trips, 1,000 sleeping tablets, a kilo of skunk, two kilos of rocky and about 300 grand in cash. This was to provide for everybody for 72 hours. Everyone knew everyone, or had at least spotted their faces at some time or another. The invitations were given out by hand and gatecrashers excluded. This was important, because word usually got around and people would go to extreme lengths to be invited. Invites could exchange hands for a long 'un or more, depending on how desperately someone wanted to go.

This particular year there was a remarkable number of strangers: including more than a few shady-looking fellas and gold-digging birds.

Roy had come to Ibiza with the wrong intentions. He'd flown over with other guests specially for this party, but hadn't got to see the birthday cake. He'd smuggled 500 duff Ecstasy tablets to Ibiza for sale to gullible users. But he wouldn't have dared sell them to Jimbo's guests, or he'd have had his arse kicked big-time.

The evening before the party, Roy had gone out in search of

eligible victims. It wasn't hard: lots of people approached him anyway. He met some guys in a club called Nightlife, who arranged to buy 100 pills at tenners. Standing at the bar, Roy sold another fifteen pills to Johnny Tourists. His unbelievable front had been learnt in prison as a teenager. As Roy waited at the bar for the 'Nightlife' guys to complete the bigger purchase, he grinned slyly as he watched people knock back his moody Es. One bloke even returned to buy another pill, claiming that the buzz was fantastic! The thing was, the tabs themselves didn't even look like real Es. They were white but had a serial number on one side, a fault that Roy sidestepped by calling them 'Convicts', adding that they packed a real motherfucking head-rush. As he grinned, he was blissfully unaware that groups of eyes were watching his every move.

Suddenly, they came at him from four directions. First he noticed a Spaniard dressed in polo shirt, blue jeans and the whitest trainers walking towards him. Roy stiffened and prepared for a confrontation, feeling easily confident enough to knock this guy right out. But as he squared up ready to fight, two other guys grabbed hold of him from each side and forced him, struggling, to the ground. Roy tried everything to break free, which upset the men even more. They beat and knocked the shit out of him, then took him outside to a waiting police mobile unit. Roy was lucky – it was an official government vehicle. If it had been rival gangsters, he would have been in big trouble.

At no time in his life had Roy been so glad to see an officer's uniform – he didn't stop to think about how much they'd hate him for selling drugs in their country. The police lost no time at all in taking him at speed back to the station. The pills were sent for analysis by a laboratory, and Roy was driven to the legendary 'Ibiza Hilton' – yeah, the local nick!

After two days he was set free, because the Es were so moody that there was nothing they could do him for. They were actually antibiotics! Roy had already told the police that the tablets were legal flu remedies for people with Ibiza flu, but his admission had been ignored. The police had been so excited about apprehending him that no one had bothered to listen, and now they wanted to beat his brains out even more for wasting police time. If he couldn't be charged with selling Ecstasy, they'd have to settle for giving him a warning and a few hard digs.

With what had already been dished out, it couldn't get much worse. Roy drove back to the villa he shared with Hoskins and Safehouse. They wouldn't have rented a villa with him, had they known he sold moody pills, but Roy had kept it to himself. Hoskins was fucked. While no one was looking, he'd sneaked home for some rest. Feeling really hungry, he'd placed a chip pan on the stove and turned the gas on full. Roy was eager to catch up with the party and asked him if he wanted a lift into town. Hoskins decided to head back into the fray, dropped everything, put some shorts and a clean shirt on and went out, to find Roy waiting impatiently on the driveway.

They drove straight to Mambo's, where most of Jimbo's headstrong guests were still hard at it. Nobody had taken any time to rejuvenate their bodies with food or sleep. The diet was purely alcohol and class-As, yet they remorselessly marched on, ignoring their bodies' natural alarm system. Still, their numbers had fallen, leaving Jimbo's bona-fide friends to bop till they literally dropped.

The whole scene was an orgy of madness and bullshit. Adam Englander – the self-proclaimed Virgina Man – was convincing everyone that the sun was moving closer to the earth, and that the planet would explode within eight months. The birthday boy himself was being chased by not one but two models, while an ex-world-champion boxer was spinning a garage set. Roy was soon boasting about beating the law; Tommy Mack was handing out champagne glasses filled with his own piss; and Mark – the daft fucker – was running round in a sarong with a 38DD bra on his small head. Peezy, Blocko and Healey had donned crash helmets, were necking tequila and began head-butting a concrete wall. Sam and Mara were nursing their friend, Kathy. Silver, Bonnie and Leanne danced on tables while everyone else chanted 'Havin' it! Havin' it!' every time someone got another round in.

As the scene descended into an inferno of Ibiza hedonism and bacchanalian excess, Hoskins had an unlikely and most unexpected thought.

## Spanish Highs

'Shit, I forgot to turn the chip pan off!'
They're probably still cleaning up after that one now!

# **24** Ibiza Epilogue

When the closing parties have all closed, and the seasons all run out of seasoning, British punters, promoters, DJs and workers reluctantly return to English soil. Most are despondent, exhausted, depressed – or all three. Staying in Ibiza for a season is almost like living someone else's reality: as you have read, it can be a dream or a nightmare. Not all Ibiza club-goers use drugs, but most do. That's the way it is. That's why people go there.

To fully analyse this chemical generation, we have to ask ourselves a number of questions: What is it that drives groups of individuals to experiment with and consume large quantities of drugs over long periods of time (i.e. the entire past decade)? What does this say about our emotional stability? Are we unhappy with our lives, emotions and personalities? Or maybe we're confused about the choices we have in life?

I've been there, seen it, done it, and am paying the price. I've seen the end of the Ecstasy rainbow and it's not a pot of gold, but a crock of shit. I won't scare or bore you with my own theories on medical and neurological difficulties for class-A users. Now that I'm drug free, I look back at those nine dedicated years of hedonism with great affection but an underlying sadness for the lifestyle I led at a time when what was really required was internal spiritual balance. Thankfully, I'm now closer than ever to reaching my goal and most satisfying of all, I'm elevating to heights that drugs could never reach.

When I returned to London from Ibiza in 1994, I founded a record company called Havin' It Records and we released an album *Havin' It In Ibiza* which reflected the club and nightlife on the island. We went on to release a total of six albums over six months and the term soon became synonymous with Ibizan clublife. We went on to book the island's oldest and most prestigious club, Pacha, for the whole of the summer of '95 and enjoyed a wild, nonstop and varied summer.

When I came back to London I hit a bit of a downer. Ibiza is so magical that arriving back at Gatwick can be a major comedown: London was fucking freezing and my mental state had been pulverised by a truckload of pharmaceuticals. I started to think heavily about who I was and what I had spent the last ten years doing.

I was young when I first threw myself into Ecstasy and we knew little, if anything, of the real dangers. But why must we pursue a rugged trail of social and personal drug abuse that can end in death or old-age misery? Can we find true ecstasy through chemically induced delirium, or is it that we are afraid to face the world as ourselves?

It is true to say that drugs do give a lot of people a temporary, but satisfying, experience. We each have our own reasons for seeking chemical fulfilment. But when the party is finally over, how do we really feel? Many drug users suffer from depression and stagnation. I myself know many people who are still doing the same things they were five to ten years ago – caning it. Not only burning the candle but chucking it in the sea. And for what?

People say that drugs open their minds, but in reality drugs only open a channel which already exists. It's just a matter of wanting to acknowledge the signs whilst on ground level, instead of addressing addled 'insights' with our heads in the clouds and our brains beneath our Es. I had a wicked time on Ibiza and I shall have a lot more – but maybe next time it'll be the real me enjoying them, without the help of chemicals. Maybe.

Trust me on this one . . .

I'll see you on the beach.